NORTH CAUCASUS DOLMENS

Boris Loza, Ph.D.

Adventures Unlimited Press

Other Books of Interest:

See more astounding science books at:
www.adventuresunlimitedpress.com

NORTH CAUCASUS DOLMENS

In Search of Wonders

Boris Loza, Ph.D.

North Caucasus Dolmens: In Search of Wonders

By Boris Loza, Ph.D.

Copyright © 2020

ISBN 978-1-948803-19-9

Published by:
Adventures Unlimited Press
One Adventure Place
Kempton, Illinois 60946 USA
auphq@frontiernet.net

AdventuresUnlimitedPress.com

Edited by L. Galanter
Front cover design by S. Zarubin
Book design by Sarah E. Holroyd (https://sleepingcatbooks.com)

10 9 8 7 6 5 4 3 2 1

NORTH CAUCASUS DOLMENS

In Search of Wonders

To my very best friends: my mom, Doba; my dad, Pavel; my wife, Galina; and my daughter, Anna.

Boris Loza was born in Krasnodar, Russia and obtained a PhD at Krasnodar University. After the dissolution of the USSR, Loza immigrated to Canada, where he lives today.

Contents

List of Figures & Tables

Introduction: Where It All Began

"Travel is fatal to prejudice, bigotry and narrow-mindedness, and many of our people need it sorely on these accounts. Broad, wholesome, charitable views of men and things cannot be acquired by vegetating in one little corner of the earth all one's lifetime."
— Mark Twain, *The Innocents Abroad*

An old proverb says, "Tell me who your friends are, and I'll tell you who you are." Although I make friends easily, family members and interesting books have always been my best friends. I'll start this book with a short story about me and my best friends.

Even as five-year-old child, I remember dreaming about adventures, such as visiting unknown places, eating exotic foods, meeting people who looked different from the people around me, experiencing foreign cultures, and studying exotic animals. In short, experiencing something completely different from what I'd always seen around myself and in the streets.

I don't know where this passion came from. Perhaps from a bedtime song my mother used to sing to me about geologists, or maybe from a large book by Czech travelers driving across Africa[1] that I found at my grandparents' house. Or perhaps it came from the beautiful sheets of animal stamps from Burundi and Guinea that I had in my personal stamp collection, exotic coins, or maybe it was just my vivid imagination and inherited curiosity. I think it was all of this together, and probably something more.

When I was in kindergarten, my maternal *babushka* (granny) used to read folk stories about *Chukchis, Koryaks,* and *Eskimos* to me.[2] This was a fascinating book about the adventures of the northern people who lived in the Bering Strait. My mind would race to far away and unknown places, and in my imagination I was the hero of these fairy tales.

When I was a child, we lived in the former Soviet Union and traveling to other countries was almost impossible for common folks like my family and me. However, my mother was fortunate enough to be able to travel to several foreign countries, which, at that time, could have been more problematic than just "raising a few eyebrows." Even now, in her 80s, she enjoys traveling, and today our daughter continues the tradition, living in other countries for up to six months. When I was her age, I couldn't dream of such things!

I have always been fascinated with the diversity and mysteries of life. In elementary school, I spent winter days in the local museum of natural history as well the city zoo. On hot summer days I would hunt for unknown and rare insects and unusual plants, and crawl on my knees and elbows in the summer puddles, turning over the bodies of dead animals seeking hidden insects and life-forms. I would make "scientific" journals in which I'd describe how they looked as well as their habitat and behaviors. I also created many collections of insects, bird feathers, minerals, plants, cactuses, and any other natural thing I could find. After completing these collections, I'd donate them to my middle school's biology class.

My favorite books at that time were an excellent seven-volume series of Russian-language books called *Life of the Animals,*[3] which was an atlas of the various insects and plants. At that time, I dreamed of becoming a biologist when I grew up. But my interests also spread to things not related to collecting insects, such as the traditions and foods of other cultures from the Krasnodar region of southern Russia.

One favorite radio show, which I never missed, was a series featuring a cute monkey, an intelligent *cachalot* (sperm whale) and a funny *gepard* (cheetah). This radio series, broadcast every other Sunday on the All-Union Radio between 1964 and 1973, used humor and stories to teach children about nature. The Russian abbreviation КОАПП ("Комитет Охраны Авторских Прав Природы") means "Committee for the Protection of Copyright of Nature."

I would also devour any book I could about travelers and adventures. Being in the Soviet Union, you couldn't find books that would ignite your imagination unless you knew someone at a bookstore. I was lucky to have the complete series of the Library of Adventure[4] at home—twenty volumes of adventure and sci-fi classics that my mother somehow got for me.

My parents supported me in all these interests. My father had always been enthusiastic about learning German and taught me German as well. Together we would go to the foreign-language bookstore, where I'd browse through the beautiful volumes of *Urania Tierreich*,[5] German-language books with beautiful photographs that would further enflame my imagination. He presented me with many interesting books and always with an inspiring personalized dedication on the first flyleaf.

Sometimes my passion for traveling would get me into trouble. Once I was on a business trip to the Primorsky Krai, a seaside region in the Far East part of Russia (at that time the Soviet Union, USSR), and I wanted to visit Nakhodka, the southernmost city in the USSR. My flight back home was in about four hours and so I bought a round-trip ticket to Nakhodka at the local bus station, figuring that a two-hour trip would be enough. In Nakhodka, I was surprised not to see even one person in civilian clothes. Everyone was dressed in military uniforms and staring at me curiously. It didn't bother me at the time, and after a while I boarded a returning bus to the airport.

After about 30 minutes of driving, we were suddenly stopped and the military border guards entered the bus. They were looking for me! One of them asked, "Where is your permit to visit the restricted military place?"

3

I was stunned to learn that I needed a special permit to visit Nakhodka and that apparently it was a restricted military zone with a strict visiting policy. At the bus station, I simply bought tickets without being asked about any permit. However, now I was prohibited from returning to the airport because I didn't have such a permit. My luggage was removed and searched, the bus moved on, and I was transferred to the military station for further investigation. I almost missed my flight home!

My first trip to a foreign country occurred after I was married and "perestroika" was just beginning in the 1980s. Anyone who wanted to travel to a foreign country still had to get approval from the local Communist Party group. The role of this group was to ask "trick" questions in order to assess your "political maturity" and readiness to travel outside the USSR, but basically, they wanted to make sure that you would return.

At the time, I was working on my PhD at Krasnodar University, so a large group of the university Communists gathered to decide if I was trustworthy enough to visit the Federal Republic of Germany (FRG, West Germany at that time) for a week. It was almost impossible at that time to buy tickets for this trip, but I was helped by my friend at the city's Central Komsomol Committee (political youth organization in the Soviet Union that all young people had to be members of, starting at a certain age).

At this Communist meeting, one person asked me the "trick" question, "Why must it be you who goes there? Everyone wants to do it." When answering this type of question, you had to be very careful because it could influence their decision about the future of your permit when they voted. I probably wasn't correct in answering this question and, after brief vote, I was denied a permit for this trip. Later, only through arbitration with my scientific director, was I finally allowed to go to the FRG.

Half a year after this trip, my daughter was born, and I was seeking a better life with more freedom, one that would allow me to pursue my passion for adventure. My entire family decided to try our luck in another country and, after living for a while in Israel, we eventually settled in Canada.

My wife, and now our daughter, always shared my passion for exploring new places and having new experiences. When you travel, you always learn more about the countries you visit—their food and customs—as well as meet local people, allowing you to form your own opinions about the many things you encounter in these places.

Sometime after emigrating to Israel, we literally dived into traveling. This was probably due to the traveling "prohibition" in the Soviet Union, so we really tried to make up for lost time. I don't know how it is now, but at that time in Israel you couldn't start traveling immediately after immigrating there unless you left a considerable amount of money as collateral in the government bank. This was in case you decided not to come back, and the money would be used to repay the government for what it had supposedly already spent on your immigration and initial support. This collateral was a must for all immigrants who had lived in the country less than three years. The Israeli government took the money quickly, but took a lot more time to give it back. Knowing all this in advance from other immigrants didn't stop us from depositing this "exit money" and going to Paris. Only after we had immigrated to Canada did traveling become more flexible and financially easy, and we could travel where and when we wanted. Everyone in my family now enjoys traveling more frequently and whenever we want to.

I've always been attracted to visiting exotic places and investigating ancient monuments built by ancient peoples. Today, no one knows (except, of course, the "omniscient" mainstream archaeologists and historians!) how ancient peoples were able to build these monuments. I've also been interested in seeing, and even participating in, various rituals and customs around the world. My heroes have always been Travelers (yes, with a capital "T") who risked their lives to visit forbidden countries and places in order to share these mysterious and out-of-the-way places with the rest of the world: Travelers like Alexandra David-Néel,[6] Ármin Vámbéry,[7] and Sir Richard Francis Burton.[8]

Traveling is collecting memories, experiences, and feelings that stay with you for the rest of your life. This may be visiting the most exotic destinations, specific historical and cultural places, or simply visiting restaurants with the best food and wine. In my opinion, unless you are young, healthy, and financially independent, one has to have some kind of strategy to get the most from a trip. My wife and I decided to "collect" unusual archaeological sites, natural wonders, interesting people and customs, strange foods, and other curiosities. We literally became addicted to traveling, seeing new places, and having new experiences. I even started learning Spanish to make traveling to South America more enjoyable.

Eventually it became such a passion that I quit a well-paid, but dull, job in a bank (and right before an announced promotion) to start living our dream (life is short!). The computer software company that I've been running for a couple of decades now pays the bills.

Outside the big city, we found a nice property in a township named after a local politician's wife's dog. This property has a large forest with lots of wild plants and a river inhabited by many interesting animals. We decided to start living healthy and green, with the goal of visiting as many interesting countries and places as possible in addition to learning more about our beautiful planet.

It's interesting that there is no official total that everyone agrees on for the number of countries in the world. The US Department of State lists only 195 independent states and the United Nation lists only 193 member states. But what, for example, about Tibet? Is it a country or part of modern China? How about Tibet's history and its unique traditions? How about Hawaii, Puerto Rico, Taiwan, and so many other previously independent countries? These countries and territories do not exist anymore, according to the US Department of State, the UN, or even the UNESCO World Heritage list.

Therefore, we decided to follow the Travelers' Century Club (TCC) list of 325 countries and territories with the intention of eventually becoming members by visiting a hundred or more countries. Although we eventually visited more than a hundred territories on the TCC list, we decided against joining the club because we do not agree with their policy that considers a plane fuel stop a visit to a country. We prefer to literally *see* countries to consider them being visited. Some countries we've visited several dozen times, others we've traveled in for a month or longer.

When I travel to a new country, I am interested in the many different things that are unique to it. This includes history, archaeology, rituals, and customs as well as local food, legends, unexplained mysteries, and strange artifacts. The *In Search of Wonders* series of books is about my own experiences, personal opinions, and impressions of the lifestyles and cultures of the places I've visited. I strongly believe that one can find many new and interesting things in any place, even if some previous visitor categorically told you that there was nothing there to see or do.

Despite the fact that English is not my native language, I have decided to write this book in English. In the West, little is known about the North Caucasus, my place of birth and where I used to live, despite its many wonders and curiosities. You can find mysterious megalithic structures there as well as the remains of ancient civilizations, similar to, for example, South America and Egypt. Although volumes have been written about other exotic countries, not many books have been written about the North Caucasus—the place I can tell you about firsthand.

The North Caucasus, or Ciscaucasia, is the northern part of the Caucasus region within European Russia, between the Sea of Azov and the Black Sea on the west and the Caspian Sea on the east. Geographically, the Northern Caucasus (the territory north of the Greater Caucasus range) includes the Russian republics of the North Caucasus (Figure 1). As part of the Russian Federation, the Northern Caucasus region is included in the North Caucasian and Southern Federal Districts and consists of Krasnodar Krai, Stavropol Krai, and the constituent republics, approximately from west to east: the Republic of Adygea, Karachay-Cherkessia, Kabardino-Balkaria, North Ossetia–Alania, Ingushetia, Chechnya, and the Republic of Dagestan. This area has many ancient megaliths (until the middle of the 19th century, large stone structures were called "Celtic monuments." Since 1863, at the suggestion of French historian-archaeologist René Galles, they began being called megaliths[9]). This book does not distinguish between different parts of the Caucasus, specifically between North Caucacus and Transcaucasus (South Caucasus). Even though this book discusses the North Caucasus dolmens, it also includes descriptions of the Transcaucasus dolmens of Abkhazia (sometimes called the Northwest Caucasus), because they are a part of the whole "map" of ancient dolmens in that area.

I am very interested in megaliths and I look for them in every country I visit. The first megaliths I saw in my life were ancient dolmens. This book is dedicated to these amazing and mystical structures. These ancient monuments, even up to the present day, remain unexplained by mainstream archaeologists and historians. Maybe they are waiting for your "discovery"?

Perhaps one does not need to travel so far to find something worth "rediscovering." Surely, in every place in the world, one may see interesting and unexplored things that have not been properly explained to someone's satisfaction.

I hope that this book will inspire a curious person to pause in the daily routine and go to an unknown place looking for the unusual and curious things that still exist in our world.

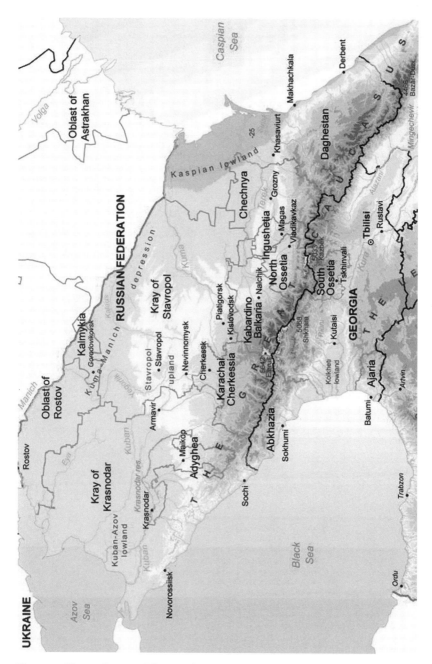

Figure 1. Physical map of the North Caucasus.

Part I

Dolmens: Ancient Mystic Megaliths

I t was common for parents in our area of the former Soviet Union to send their children to a "pioneer camp" by the Black Sea for a month or more, apparently for the health benefits. I used to spend several months a year in these camps.

I remember seeing strange megalithic structures in the woods when we were wandering around the camp on our own. They looked pretty ancient to me, and many were already befouled with graffiti and human excrement inside or near the structures. Later, I learned that such structures were called *dolmens*.

North Caucasus Dolmens

According to the *Oxford English Dictionary*, a 1754 book on Cornish antiquities indicates that the current term in the Cornish language for a *cromlech* (Welsh dolmen or underground tomb) was *tolmen* ("hole of stone"). The dictionary also indicates that this term was inexactly reproduced by Théophile Malo Corret de La Tour d'Auvergne as *dolmin* and was used by French archaeologists for *cromlech* (a group of megaliths, sometimes arranged in a circle or in concentric circles).[1]

Another theory is that the word *dolmen* is of Breton origin. It consists of two roots, *taol* (table) and *maen* (rock). Breton, or Old French, is still the language of the Celtic population in Brittany, the northwestern province of France, which rightfully could be called a country of megaliths (large stones). In the 17th century, the Breton language was used to name the main megalithic structures: stone circle (*crom llech*), long stone–menhir (*maen-hir*), and stone table (*taol maen*).[2]

The North Caucasus dolmens are different from what is normally called a *dolmen* in other countries and could be better described as ancient megalithic structures (Figure 2). However, in this text we will call them *dolmens*, as they are called in Russia.

Figure 2. Left, a 1967 photo of a dolmen near Azanta village, Abkhazia; right, a typical dolmen in the Gelendzhik area (Pshada village).

The Adyghe mountain people (*Adyghe* is the native name of the Circassians) considered dolmens as sacred structures, and revered and protected them. They called them "dwarf houses" (*ispun*). The Cossacks who came here later called dolmens "heroic huts," "granddads," "house of the Bogatyrs" (Figure 3), or "devils' huts."[3]

The Adyghe people still consider the territory where the dolmens are found to be sacred. Local people did not build houses in this area for a long time and visited the dolmens only in extreme cases, when they wanted to ask them about something important. If one's desire is strong, sincere, and, most importantly, good, it will certainly come true. Any mistrust or sarcasm when visiting a dolmen is perceived as a personal insult, and the dolmen can severely punish a wicked or mer-

Figure 3. Dolmen near the city of Gelendzhik at the beginning of the 20th century (1900–1917) on an old postcard. The postcard text says: "Ancient stone house of the Bogatyrs." Bogatyr in Russian folklore is someone who is big and very strong, like the Roman god Hercules.

cenary person, or turn away people who question the dolmen's sacredness.

The dolmens of the Caucasus range from the Taman Peninsula to the Colchis Lowlands, a distance of about 480 km long (about 300 miles) and from 30 to 75 km wide (about 19 to 47 miles). The Western Caucasus (the Abkhazia, Krasnodar, and Stavropol territories of Russia) is known to have about 2,300 dolmens (Figure 4), of which only 20 percent have survived in their original state. To date, archaeologists have excavated about 160 of these dolmens.[4]

The vast majority of the dolmens belong to the so-called "tiled" type. They are made up of large stone slabs, four of which are erected vertically and covered by a fifth slab, forming the roof of a stone box or dolmen chamber. The front slab is always taller than the rear slab, so that the roof of the dolmen is tilted back. The slabs are carefully adjusted to each other with the help of special grooves and protrusions. The front

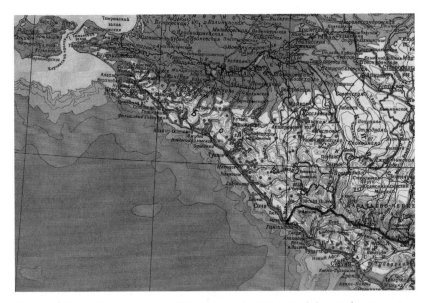

Figure 4. Map of the dolmens of the Krasnodar Krai. Red dots indicate groups of dolmens.

slab of the dolmen has a small round, oval, or (rarer) more complex hole (archaeologists call it a *manhole*). We will call it the *entrance hole* in the text, emphasizing its utilitarian purpose (however, there were once dolmens in the Caucasus without a hole. Unfortunately, almost all of them are currently destroyed. In this book, we will only discuss dolmens with a hole).

Sometimes a sixth plate slab was used to form the floor of the dolmen chamber, but more often the dolmens were placed directly on the soil or on special stones (so-called "heel stones"). The multitonnage slabs from which the dolmens were made are in their original state, that is, not processed. However, on the surface of the inside chamber, the stone is carefully leveled, sometimes even polished.

The dolmens usually stand in groups along river basins. Orientation of the dolmens in the terrain is different, but as a rule the orientation fits into the arc of the sunrise and sunset, as well as the culmination of heavenly bodies. That is, the dolmen entrance holes usually face east, west, northeast, northwest, or south. Only single monuments face north.

Radiocarbon analysis shows that the North Caucasian dolmens were built between 2700 and 1400 BC, making them 3,400 to 4,700 years old. However, this dating method is unreliable and can only determine the minimum age of the dolmens.

Nobody knows today who built the dolmens, or how, when, and for what purpose. Archaeological finds from the dolmens and individual settlements allow us to speak about the high culture of their builders. There is evidence that dolmens emanate some unknown power, although what kind of energy it is and how they do it is a mystery. We will try to discover answers to this and other mysteries, based on a dolmen's connection with other similar structures around the world as well as other evidence.

Properties of the Dolmens

North Caucasus dolmens have a perfect shape, and the inner chamber and the entrance hole have specific mathematical proportional ratios. The blocks are connected with great precision. According to some sources, each stone block can weigh between three and eight metric tons (one metric ton is a unit of weight equal to 1,000 kg),[5] however, other sources indicate weights up to 30 metric tons.[6]

Dolmens come in different shapes and sizes, but all of them are enclosed structures, usually built with rectangular megalithic flat blocks that are fitted together well. No writing in any form has been found on the dolmens, although some of them are covered inside and outside with geometric carvings. It is unusual that the early stages of dolmen development and their evolution cannot be traced—from more primitive forms and technology to advanced ones—but sophisticated, complex dolmens appeared instantaneously.

An important element of dolmen construction is the entrance hole in the front wall. It is located on the centerline of the front wall and at a specific height from the base. The most common position is the center of the hole, which divides the front wall in height in a proportion of 1:2 (from the bottom up), less often in a proportion of 3:4. This hole has the form of a circle, a semicircle, an ovoid, or a rectangle (rare). The horizontal size of the hole (diameter of the circle, semicircle, etc.) is usually 40 cm (1.3 ft.).[7]

With all the variety in dolmen sizes, the angles of the inclination of the chambers are sustained. The angle of the horizontal inclination of the chamber is about 94.4 degrees, and the slope of the roof is about 95.4 degrees.[8] Statistically, the average North Caucasian dolmen has the following characteristics:

- Perimeter of the base of the chamber is 720 cm (23.6 ft.)[9]
- Angle of the chamber is 94.4 degrees
- Slope of the roof is 95.4 degrees
- Entrance hole in the front wall is about 40 cm (1.3 ft.) in diameter and is shaped in a circle whose center is on the centerline of the front wall, dividing it in a 1:2 proportion (from the bottom up)
- Average length is 3 m (9.8 ft.)
- Average width is about 2 m (6.6 ft.)
- Average height is around 2 m (6.6 ft.)
- Average weight of a single dolmen is about 20 metric tons

The dolmens were composed of various materials, depending on the terrain: sandstone, sandy limestone, and, less often, granite, silicic, and metamorphic rocks.

Dolmen Differences

Some dolmens are rectangular in shape (Figure 5) and made of five or six blocks, others are composite (Figure 6) (made of many pieces), some are rock-hewn monoliths (Figure 7), and others have a sarcophagus-like shape (Figure 8)—but all have a hole in the front panel.

Rock-hewn dolmens were constructed partially or completely from the existing rock. Note that the interior chamber of this type of dolmen had to be built (in case of the complete monoliths) through the small entrance hole at the front wall. No other access to the interior chamber of the dolmen was possible.

Figure 5. Example of a tiled-type rectangular dolmen (dolmen in the Gelendzhik area).

Figure 6. Example of a composite dolmen (dolmen in the Gelendzhik area).

Figure 7. Rock-hewn dolmens were constructed from the existing rock of the mountain (dolmen in Lazarevsky City District of Sochi near Soloniki village).

Figure 8. Sarcophagus-like dolmen with broken lid (dolmen in Geojtam tract, Ashe River basin).

Figure 9. Examples of dolmen plugs (Gelendzhik area).

The holes at the front could be closed with a phallic-shaped stone plug (Figure 9) weighing up to 150 kg (330.7 lbs.).[10]

Most of the few plugs remaining today are quite large and heavy, even for one person to lift. The size of the hole for the plug ranges from .30 to .45 m (11.8–17.7 inches) and the length can reach up to 1 m (39.37 in.).[11]

Dolmen "Volkonsky" (Figures 10 and 11) is the only surviving full-size, monolithic-type dolmen, that is, its camera is completely carved into the rock through a small inlet. It is located at the gorge of the God-lyk River, in the village of Volkonka, and is a popular tourist site protected by the state.

Almost all dolmens have round entrance hole. However about 1 percent of dolmens have square or arcuate shapes for the entrance hole (Figure 12).

 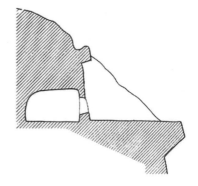

Figure 10. Left, famous rock-hewn Volkonsky dolmen on the river Godlyk; right, the cut of the Volkonsky dolmen.

Figure 11. Set of stamps issued to commemorate 2014 Olympic Games in Sochi.

Figure 12. Examples of dolmens with different shapes for the entrance hole. Statistically, 99 percent of dolmens have a round entrance (left, Tuapse area; right, Fars River, north of Novosvobodnaya village).

Figure 13. Examples of dolmens with a "false" plug (left, Tuapse area; right, Mezeguh ridge at the right bank of the Ashe River).

Many dolmens have a so-called "false" plug (no through-hole), sometimes even together with a "real hole" and a plug on another side (Figure 13).

Dolmen blocks were fit together with high precision, which was remarkable for Neolithic people with apparently only primitive tools (Figure 14).

Figure 14. Dolmens with interlocking walls (dolmen in Sochi area; inset, dolmen in Psebe village, Tuapse area).

Many dolmens are decorated with sophisticated bas-reliefs and geometric patterns (Figures 15 and 16).

Figure 15. Dolmens with decorative geometric patterns or bas-reliefs (left, dolmen in the village of Vozrozhdenie on the Janet River); right, dolmen in the Wide Gap in Gelendzhik area).

Figure 16. Decorations inside of the dolmens (left, dolmen in the village of Vozrozhdenie; right, dolmen in Gelendzhik area).

Several dolmens have spacious courtyards (Figure 17).

Figure 17. Examples of dolmens with courtyards (left, dolmen in Dzhubga village; right, dolmen on the Janet River).

Some anomalous dolmens have two or more through-holes, or even no holes at all, and may have been reconstructed later using parts from several dolmens.

Studies have shown that all dolmens are near water sources. The presence of water sources near dolmens is noted by researchers of West European megaliths,[12] and a river, stream, or spring is located 5–50 m (16.4–164.0 ft.) away.[13] Even if the dolmen is on a slope or at the top of a mountain, there is a nearby water source, sometimes underground.

Few dolmens contained human remains or human parts. Some dolmens had fragments of ceramics and bones from domesticated animals near the front plate. However, this does not prove that dolmens were built for burial purposes, as not all dolmens have human remains and, therefore, dolmens cannot be classified as ancient tombs. These remains could have been placed there at a later time.

The skeletons of the human remains were found in what we call the fetal position, in which the human bones are unnaturally close to each other. This could have an important meaning for ancient peoples, who may have believed that people must leave this world in the same position they were born in (burying in the fetal position for this reason exists in other cultures, such as in Tibet).

Next to the deceased were found his belongings, stone and bronze tools, as well as utensils made of gray clay. After conquering the Caucasus, Russians noticed that "Shapsugs" (one of the twelve tribes of the Circassian, or Adyghe, people) used to bring sacrificial food to some of the dolmens.[14]

To be clear, there has been little progress in answering any of the sacramental questions of who, how, when, and why various megaliths were built. This is due to a lack of any epigraphs on the structures, except for some runes and other marks made much later and not by the original builders. However, some zigzag lines and spirals were carved into the stone at the time of construction, which will be discussed later. This book will attempt to answer the sacramental questions of who, how, when, and why, at least for the North Caucasus dolmens.

Who Built the Dolmens

On the "mighty meadow" (*bogatyrskaya polyana*) near the village of Novosvobodnaya, 360 dolmens were once lined up in regular rows, resembling the streets of a small village.[1] Not without reason, local ethnic groups such as the Adyghe people called them *ispun*, "dwarfs" (little people) houses; the Abkhaz called them *keuz* and *adamara*, "ancient burial dwellings"; whereas the Megrelians named them *mdishkude, odzvale,* or *sadavale,* "dwellings of the giants."[2]

Gnomes (or dwarfs) and giants exist in the mythology of almost all peoples around the world. For example, in Scandinavian mythology, gnomes live in stone or under the earth and turn into stone if they are exposed to sunlight. Old Icelandic even has a special verb that means "to turn into stone, being caught by the dawn."[3]

Giants are analogous to dwarfs but are mentioned somewhat less than gnomes. Collectively, the individuality of giants and gnomes is primarily formed from their size, specifically their large size. Giants are the most ancient creatures, older than life, and are hostile to life. They live in mountains and deserts and themselves are semi-human, semi-mountainous.[4]

An interesting fact is that most of the legends about dolmens are associated with some kind of mysterious dwarf people. There are the *isps* in the Nart saga of the Adyghe people, the *atsany* of the Abkhazians, the *bitsenta* of the Ossetians, and the *iebany* in the mythology of the African Dogon tribe (also well-known builders of dolmens in the distant past).

Dwarf people in India used to live in the mountains. Interesting information about these very evil and ugly dwarfs who engaged in witchcraft can be found in H. P. Blavatsky's *The People of the Blue Mountains*.[5] According to Ossetian legends, dwarfs called the *bitsenta* people came from the sea (they literally lived in the sea) and settled in the North Caucasus area. They had unique abilities and could knock down a tree with a glance, move cliffs, and talk to each other hundreds of kilometers away. Perhaps they came from across the sea, that is, from India?

One Adyghe legend claims that many years ago mighty giants and gnomes existed. The giants lived in river valleys and hunted, and the gnomes lived high in the snowy mountains in dark, cold caves and engaged in witchcraft. They also rode on harnessed hares. The giants, though being strong, were foolish, like a herd of sheep. The gnomes, despite having absolutely no power, were very cunning. The two tribes lived for a long time not seeing and not knowing about each other. But one day, the gnomes descended into the valley and saw the giants playing games, throwing rocks at each other, and tearing out trees by their roots. The tiny gnomes, through cunning and witchcraft, soon managed to conquer the stupid giants and forced them to serve the gnomes. Ordered by the dwarfs, the giants quickly agreed to start working on building small huts (*ispuns*) everywhere in the mountains and valleys. These huts had small, round holes through which only one gnome could get inside (Figure 18).

Another legend tells a different story about the dolmens. The indigenous inhabitants of the North Caucasus, the people who lived in the mountains, used to live for so long that they literally dried up, turned into babies, and were reborn again. These old men were allegedly placed into stone boxes in which they received a new life. Thus, the soul did not leave its body, only the body "shell" changed. Celtic legends associated with the

Figure 18. Illustration from the 1660 book Korte Beschryvinge Van eenige Vergetene en Verborgene Antiquiteten showing giants building dolmens for dwarfs.

fairy people also describe dolmens as gateways to another world—elves whose ancestral home, according to researchers, was the North Caucasus.

Many water images are depicted both inside and outside dolmens. It is quite possible that the territory of the Caucasus was destroyed in ancient times from the Great Flood. This can be evidenced by the ancient Caucasian legends (such as about Dzerassa, a daughter of the water god Donbettyr in the Nart saga of the Ossetians). Some toponyms tell the story: in the Kuban region (were dolmens are located), the name "Kuban" in Adyghe is *Pshize* and is derived from *pshi*, "water," and *ze*, "once." That is, it once was water.[6]

The Adyghe people also called dolmens "houses of eternity," and according to popular belief, dwarfs did not go away but descended underground and lived in caves. Sometimes they come up to the surface, and then strange things occurred in the dolmens. Over their stone houses, mysterious lights are lit, and at times sounds resembling thunder rolls are heard. Therefore, the Adyghe people never settle near dolmens and try to avoid them.

Today there are about 2,300 known dolmens in the Caucasus, however, some researchers estimate that the original number of dolmens could have been as high as 30,000.[7] Dolmens are not only found in Russia; dolmen-like megalithic structures are found in Europe, America, Africa, and southeast Asia (Figure 19).

Figure 19. Old photos of dolmens in Bagneux, France, and in the Merina region, Madagascar, Africa.

Korea leads in the number of dolmens, and before the start of the Second World War, Korea had as many as 80,000 man-made stone structures; today only about 30,000 remain.[8]

Volumes have been written about the mystery of Stonehenge. According to conventional archaeology, Stonehenge was built at approximately the same time as the North Caucasus dolmens; the building blocks of the dolmens weigh about the same as the building blocks of Stonehenge—around 20 metric tons.

Something does not fit here. We imagine that the man of the primitive communal clan society, who built megalithic structures, lived in relatively small groups, and was limited by the possibilities of subsistence provided by hunting, harvesting, and shepherding. Such a primitive mode of existence required a considerable territory for every kind of group or tribe. Where did the human forces necessary for such colossal construction activities come from? Where did the hundreds of strong men who could move Stonehenge stones come from? We can ask the same questions about the builders of dolmens.

First Attempts to Study Dolmens

In 1802, zoologist and botanist Peter Simon Pallas published notes about his travels to "the edge" of the Russian empire.[9]

Among other unusual things, he also mentioned dolmens. In 1818, Edouard Taitbout de Marigny, a French sailor in the Russian service, recorded a group of six dolmens on the Pshada River. During the Caucasian War in 1830, British intelligence officer James Bell, who lived among the Shapsugs, made scenic sketches of mountain people against the background of dolmens. Dubois de Montpéreux continued studying dolmens in North Caucasus and in Crimea in 1833 (Figure 20). Bayern Friedrich Samoilovich, a natural scientist and archaeologist, in 1871 published a book in which he described dolmens and included his drawings (Figure 21).[10]

In the second half of the 19th century, the North Caucasus dolmens were thoroughly studied and described in detail.

Figure 20. First drawings of dolmens by Dubois de Montpéreux in the Crimea near Gaspra, and at Fort St. Nicholas near Poti, Georgia.

Archaeologists did not find any tools or construction support that might have been used for building these megalithic structures. They were surprised to see that the construction blocks were carefully leveled and treated, sometimes covered with carved patterns and rarely painted. Some dolmens were built using several stones instead of a one big plate. In all cases, the stones were fit so precisely together that there was not even the smallest gap between blocks.

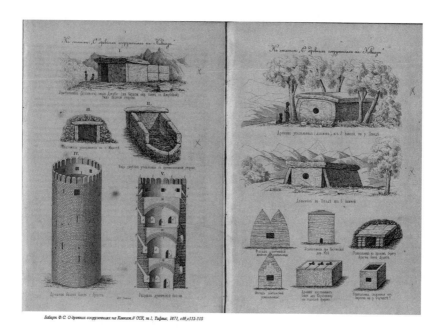

Figure 21. Drawings of dolmens Bayern Friedrich Samoilovich published in 1871.

Several experiments were conducted to prove that ancient people could create these structures. The construction of dolmens was extremely difficult and complex, taking into account the primitive techniques of the Neolithic and Bronze Ages. This is clearly demonstrated by such a case, quoted by A. A. Formozov. In 1960 it was decided by the employees of the Abkhazian Museum to transport one dolmen from Escheri to Sukhumi to the courtyard of the Abkhazian Museum (I emphasize: do not build a new dolmen, but transport the old one a relatively short distance by truck along a good motorway). They chose the smallest dolmen and use a crane on it, but no matter how they fastened the loops of the steel cables on the cover slab, it did not move. They brought in a second crane, and while the two cranes were able to lift the heavy monolith, which weighed many tons, it was too much to lift it to the truck. For one year the dolmen's roof lay waiting in Escheri, while in Sukhumi they searched for a more powerful crane. In 1961, with the help of a new machine, all the stones were loaded onto trucks. But the

31

most important thing was still ahead: to reassemble the structure. A long time passed before it was possible, and the trees of the museum garden had been taken down, and one wall of the dolmen was broken. And yet the reconstruction was only partially implemented. The roof was lowered onto the four walls, but they could not move it so that its edges sat in the grooves on the inner surface of the roof. In ancient times, the plates fit so well together that it was impossible to insert a knife blade between the blocks. Now there was a big gap.[11]

Because of this precision, attempts to move and later reconstruct dolmens were unsuccessful. For example, repeated attempts by archaeologists to reconstruct a round dolmen on the Janet River in the North Caucasus failed (Figure 22). The finished blocks collapsed and there are gaps of several centimeters between the blocks. This is not due to the archaeologists' incompetence or carelessness but because the base of the dolmen was destroyed, so precisely fitting the blocks into the original position was impossible.

Figure 22. Photo of the round dolmen on the Janet River at the beginning of the 20th century before its destruction in 1950. Note the vertical gaps between the blocks before (left) and after (right) the reconstruction in 1998.

Dolmen Anatomy

Dolmens share several common characteristics:[12]
- Typically built in rows with a common embankment

- Installed on a leveled platform, especially noticeable on slopes
- Usually located at elevations of 250–400 m (820–1,315 ft.) above sea level, less often from 400–800 m (1,315–2,630 ft.), sometimes more than 800 m (2,630 ft.)
- Entrance holes closed by a plug, although some rare dolmens have no holes
- Usually located with the entrance hole facing a river; most with the orientation to the southeast or south
- Symmetry of dimensions—the presence of several standard sizes, that is, scale
- Inner surfaces of the blocks are usually leveled or ground
- Zigzag or spiral scratched lines sometimes appear on the walls

Typically, a stand-alone dolmen consists of six sandstone blocks (Figure 23) that are fit together (except dolmens that are rock-hewn). One plate is at the base, four blocks are around the base, and one block is on the top. According to some modern researchers of dolmens, 92 percent of all dolmens are built with only five or six blocks.[13]

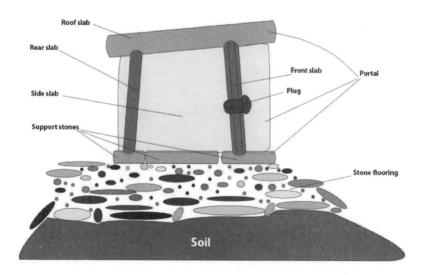

Figure 23. Sectional drawing of a dolmen showing a simplified scheme of slabs and installed on stone flooring.

The cover plate could weigh between 15 and 30 metric tons, and other blocks could weigh between 3 and 8 metric tons. The average size of North Caucuses dolmens is 3 m (9.84 ft.) long, 2 m (6.56 ft.) wide, and 2 m (6.56 ft.) high. The diameter of the round hole on the front plate is between 30 cm (0.98 ft.) and 45 cm (1.47 ft.).[14] A few dolmens have rectangular entrance holes.

Looking at the similarities with other structures in other locations, we can form some theories about who built the dolmens. Table 1 compares similar dolmen technologies around the world.

Table 1. Comparison of dolmen construction features around the world

Feature	North Caucasus dolmen	Location of similar technology	Other locations
Heavy megalithic blocks weighing several tons are used for construction.	Maya dolmen near the village of Pshada	Bagneux, France	Around the world (South America, Europe, Asia)
Sandstone is the primary material for construction blocks.	Dolmen on the Janet River	Tiwanaku, Bolivia	Around the world
Construction blocks have a very smooth surface.	Dolmen in Gelendzhik	Pyramids of Giza, Egypt	Around the world

Feature	North Caucasus dolmen	Location of similar technology	Other locations
Curved brickwork. This kind of brickwork enhances tolerance against earthquakes.	Dolmen on the Janet river	Cuzco, Peru	South America, Egypt, China, India, Malta, Turkey, and other locations
Bas-relief style. The whole plate is specially treated so that the entire surface is removed except for the protruding ornament.	Dolmen in "Shirokaja Shel" (Wide Gap) in Gelendzhik district	La-Roche district, France	Europe, South America, Egypt, China, India, and other locations
Geometric patterns on the surface of the blocks.	Dolmen on the Archuz River, Karachay-Cherkess Republic	Newgrange, Ireland	Scotland, Ireland, Europe, South America, Egypt, China, India, and other locations

Feature	North Caucasus dolmen	Location of similar technology	Other locations
Precision of construction blocks. Impossible to squeeze even a razor blade between the gaps in the blocks.	Dolmen "Klady 3" near village of Novosvobodnaya	Cusco, Peru	South America, Egypt, China, India, and other locations
Grooves and slots for connecting blocks.	Dolmen near Pshada village	Puma Punku, Bolivia	South America, Europe, Scotland, Ireland, Malta, and other locations
Rock-hewn dolmens.	Dolmen Volkonsky near Tuapse city	Ollantaytambo, Peru	South America, Egypt, China, India, and other locations

Feature	North Caucasus dolmen	Location of similar technology	Other locations
No writing of any kind found, although some blocks have simple effigies.	Stand-alone dolmen on the Janet River	Tarxien, Malta	South America, Europe, Scotland, Ireland, Malta, and other locations
"Soft" stone technology. Some blocks look like they're made of plastic that later became "hard as stone."	Dolmen in district of Novyy ("new") village	Cusco, Peru	South America, Egypt, China, India, and other locations
Specific interlocking technique for joining blocks.	Dolmen No 54, Kizinka River	Pyramids of Giza, Egypt	Around the world
Bosses (in architecture, a boss is a knob or protrusion of stone). They are not ornamental features.	Dolmen in Dzhubga village	Ollantaytambo, Peru	Around the world

I would like to point out that the bosses are such a ubiquitous feature of the megaliths found around the world, that famous Catalonian archi-

Figure 24. Bosses of a symbolic megalithic structure in the Sagrada Familia in Barcelona, Spain.

tect Antoni Gaudí used them in a small symbolic replica of a megalithic structure at the Passion Facade of the Sagrada Familia in Barcelona, Spain. With this replica, he probably wanted to say that the origins of contemporary architecture have an ancient megalithic ancestry (Figure 24).

Another peculiarity is that some dolmens are made in the so-called "Cusco style," which is a trapezoidal structure (Figure 25).

In the Leso-Kyafar area of the Karachay-Cherkess Republic, one of the dolmens stands apart from the others and is particularly interesting (Figure 26).

This dolmen is located less than 60 km (40 miles), as the crow flies, from the main North Caucasus dolmens location. It is built with polygonal masonry, the same as many ancient structures in South America and other places around the world (Figure 27).

Figure 25. Trapezoid-shaped dolmens compared to the Inca style of structures in Cusco.

Figure 26. The Leso-Kyafar area of the Karachay-Cherkess Republic provides an example of polygonal masonry in dolmen construction, which is another connection with ancient structures around the world.

H. P. Blavatsky considered these similar stone monoliths as the last relics of the Atlanteans. Based on similarities in the above examples of ancient architecture, we can say that dolmens also belong to the structures made by the so-called "Atlantean League," the ancient civilization of Atlanteans.[15]

In addition to a similar technology for building megaliths, several important characteristics are essential to the culture found among ancient megalithic peoples (based on G. Eremin 1979).[16]

Figure 27. Megaliths in the painting *Death of Atlantis*, by Russian painter Nicholas Roerich. This work is known in the English world as The Last of Atlantis, 1928 or 1929.

- **Associated structures.** In addition to dolmens in the North Caucasus, one can find menhirs and cromlechs scattered around.
- **Proximity to the sea.** The Caucasus megaliths and dolmens are always built close to a water source. Some authors even suggest that dolmens were built by people who migrated from the shores of the Black Sea. As discussed later in the book, the area where dolemns are located today may have been closer to the sea or even covered by water in ancient times.
- **Celestial orientation.** Another sign of megalithic culture is specific astral orientation to important celestial objects, such as the sun, moon, and some constellations. This is discussed later in the book in relation to the dolmens.
- **Ores and metal mines.** Megalithic cultures are attracted to areas rich in metals, particularly copper and tin deposits and associated constituents of bronze alloys (such as antimony and arsenic). In 1961, on Mount Pastukhova near Arkhyz, geologists found ancient Bronze Age copper ore mines on the slope of the mountain at an altitude of 2,500 m (8,202 ft.) above sea level.
- **Legends about giants and dwarfs.** Where there are megaliths there are also legends about the giants who built them. Dwarfs are also popular characters in legends about giants, and dolmens have their share of these legends.
- **Similar ethnographic and folklore rituals.** Adyghe, Circassians, and Abkhazians of the western Black Sea region, like people in other megalithic places, have cults around a goat (in other cultures it's a bull, ram, or deer) and ritual sacrifices of these animals dedicated to the sky, the sun, or lightning. They also had ancient fights and "games" with bulls as well as fire rituals. These "megalithic dances"—English Morris dancing, Basque dances with swords, Caucasian "dances with sabers," and especially male "dances" in the Caucasus and Basque Country—are also very peculiar.
- **Similar protolanguage.** G. Eremin argues that another feature of megalithic cultures is the existence of "secret" or "sacred" lan-

guages spoken by men (hunters, warriors, priests) (Eremin 1979). Similar secret languages existed at the beginning of this century among the Adyghe and Abkhazians. Researchers call them "hunting" and "military" languages. For example, the ancient Adyghe people (Kabardians and Circassians) had several such strange languages: *farshishe, shakobshe, zikovshire,* and others. Today, these languages have been lost. Scientists who studied some of the sacred languages that still exist in other parts of the world can distinguish the names of ancient Sumerian gods, the creators of the first civilization according to "official" history.[17] Could it be that, like the Bible says, in ancient times all people once spoke the same language (at a time when one technology existed for building megaliths)?

- **Matriarchate.** Rule by women and a cult of the mother goddess are found in the megalithic cultures of Western Europe, North Africa, the Caucasus, and South India. The influence of matriarchy can be seen today in the beliefs, legends, and customs of various nations. The Abkhazians and Adyghe have various names for the mother of the legendary Narts: Sataney-Guasha (sometimes she is called by other names: Gunda, Ahumida, Anana-Gunda, Dzgara-Guna, and others).[18]

- **Building megaliths in seismically active areas.** All dolmens were built in such places, as discussed in the "Progress-Boosting Technology and Baby-Making Machine" section.

According to mainstream historians and archaeologists, the earliest human civilization existed in Sumer, in the southernmost region of ancient Mesopotamia (modern-day Iraq and Kuwait), between 4000 and 3100 BC. According to various definitions, civilization is considered an advanced state of human society in which a high level of culture, science, industry, and government has been reached.

Sumerians did not build monolithic structures, and their building materials of choice were mud bricks or, later, fired bricks (Figure 28). Their statues were carved from imported stone. As Table 1 shows, dol-

Figure 28. An example of Sumerian architecture. The entire shape and look of the Sumerian ziggurat may look similar to some megaliths, but it is not constructed with megalithic blocks.

men constructions with similar characteristics exist around the world. But Sumerian structures did not have these characteristics and its marks are not present in other parts of the world.

Although modern archaeologists and historians don't believe any civilizations existed before Sumer, similarity of architecture and construction styles around the globe suggest the opposite. Many alternative researchers say that the Atlantean, that is, the antediluvian, advanced civilization preceded all others. More information about the existing evidence of this civilization from around the world can be seen in the Lost Cities series of books.[19]

Like the Sumerian civilization, dolmen builders required a well-organized society. How many men and women needed to be engaged in hunting, cattle breeding, defense, and maintenance of the economic infrastructure to support the large group of people and the construction necessary to create such magnificent megaliths? This was possible only in a society with a state organization and a well-organized economic infrastructure. Therefore, in my opinion, the people who built the dolmens (and other megaliths around the world) were a different civilization that existed before Sumer, that is, the Atlanteans! If not them, then another highly developed civilization that had spread around the world and has been lost to history.

Elongated Skull Connection

Another interesting connection exists between megaliths and elongated skulls. Elongated skulls have also been found in many world cultures and around the globe, including the North Caucasus. Some cultures artificially deformed skulls by distorting the normal growth of a child's skull with the help of prolonged use of mechanical action. This tradition existed not only in distant historical epochs but also in comparatively recent times and in several regions, for example in Vanuatu. However, elongated skulls were found in unborn fetuses. Many alternative researchers hypothesize that these skulls belonged to an extinct race of people with elongated skulls, who influenced later populations to practice artificial cranial deformation.

The Russian newspaper *Komsomolskaja Pravda* reported on September 4, 2016, about the burial of "long-headed" people who had been found in Kabardino-Balkaria (the Kabardino-Balkaria Republic, KBR, borders Karachay-Cherkessia on the west, where the Leso-Kyafar dolmen is located. See Figure 26 above and Figure 29). According to the newspaper:

"In the ancient necropolis above the village of Zayukovo excavations have been going on since 2011," says Viktor Kotlyarov, head of the Russian Geographical Society in the KBR [Kabardino-Balkaria]. This year, a burial site was discovered that contained the skeleton of a person with a deformed skull—a girl about 16 years old. The skull was well-preserved and all the teeth were available. This appeared to be a Sarmatian burial of the third to fourth century AD. A second elongated skull was also found, but it is not yet possible to say who it is of, as its condition was much worse. A couple of years ago, several elongated skulls were found nearby on the east side of the village of Kendelen.

These are not the first elongated skulls. The National Museum of the KBR contains many burials of humans found with elongated skulls in the KBR. Konstantin Chkheidze, the author of books about Kabarda and Balkaria, believes there is a connection between Kabarda and ancient Egypt, where this practice also existed. However, elongated skulls have also been found in South and North America, and the Maya people practiced this until quite recently.

Figure 29. Elongated skull found in Kabardino-Balkaria.

Close to the Caucasus, elongated skulls have been found in Crimea (about a four-hour drive from the North Caucasus) and in Central Asia (Figure 30).

So the question of who built the dolmens remains unanswered. Another good question is *why* the dolmens were built in the first place?

Figure 30. Elongated skull in the Historical Museum of Tajikistan in Dushanbe.

Why the Dolmens Were Built

M any theories and much speculation exist regarding the purpose of dolmens. As we have seen, dolmens were probably built by antediluvian civilizations and their purpose has been lost in ancient history. Knowledge that is part of a relatively small group of people can be lost, however, beliefs that are part of our nature belong to much a bigger group and can continue to exist even after such disasters as the Great Flood.

Since human remains were not found in every dolmen, we can safely discard the theory that the dolmens were built as burial places or tombs. In this chapter, I want to explore some possible theories for the existence of dolmens.

Tree of Life

From ancient times, people have worshiped trees, something that probably goes back to the time of the Sumerians. Immortality for the Sumerians was associated with the "tree of life" (*Giš.Ig*[1]), which they looked for everywhere and which was depicted in iconography throughout their civilization. Images of the tree of life are found in almost all cultures.

Trees with good qualities were worshiped, altars were built in the hollows of such trees, and gifts were offered. Before appealing to the "sacred" tree with a request, it was watered, given presents (tied up with fragments of bright cloth, or sweets were hung on the branches). People suffering from various ailments were led through the hollow of the sacred tree or passed through the sacred groves, and herds of animals would be taken through them to protect them from diseases and death.

Some strong trees were considered extremely powerful. It was even believed that spending the night under certain trees could, allegedly, take away a person's life force. Many beliefs are associated with the fruits of trees, which greatly extend the life of a person or endow him or her with some important abilities.

The connection between humans and plants is deep. Our DNA is likely more similar than different from plants. For example, we share approximately 60 percent of our DNA with a banana plant. We can even get virus infections from plants and vice versa. Epidermodysplasia verruciformis (EV) is an extremely rare skin disease that occurs when wartlike lesions cover parts of the body, and many of these lesions take on the appearance of tree bark or tree roots. Because of this, EV is sometimes referred to as "tree-man syndrome" (Figure 31).

Figure 31. A person suffering from tree-man syndrome.

The North Caucasus does not have many trees with large enough trunks or tree hollows. What if the dolmen served as a representation of the tree? Water is always near the dolmen (symbolizing the watering of the tree). There is almost always a round entrance in the front of the dolmen into which a living person can squeeze with arms extended forward. What if the dolmen entrance represented a tree hollow? A person in need had to pass through it to get healing for ailments or to fulfill desires. It was believed that energy was collected inside the dolmen, in its hollow space, and this energy was very intense. As we will see later in the book, this energy was used for healing purposes and for influencing people's behavior.

Talking Stones

Atlanteans viewed the earth as a living organism and the planet Earth as a part of the universe, with all life connected with the Universal Mind. Ancient peoples built megalithic structures in special places, or power points, along the earth's energy grid, thereby enhancing universal energy flows. What if dolmens, even today, continue to function as data communicators with the universe?

There is much evidence in ancient manuscripts about the stones speaking to humans. A. Aseev writes in his work *About Megalithic Constructions of the Ancient World*:

H. P. Blavatsky, in the second volume of her book "The Secret Doctrine" refers to the extensive work of De Mirville: "Memoires adressees aux Academies," which collected historical evidence that in ancient times, in the days of miracles, both pagan and biblical stones moved, spoke, and uttered prophecies, and even sang.... In "Achaicus" we see how Pausanius admits that in the beginning of his work he considered Greeks to be very stupid for their "worship of the stones." But when he reached Arcadia, he adds, "I've changed my mind." Because without worshiping stones or stone idols and statues, which are one and the same—a crime for which the Catholic Church of Rome unreasonably reproached the Gentiles—you may be allowed to believe what so many great philosophers and holy men believed, and not deserve the nickname "idiot" by modern Pausanius.

Readers are invited to apply to the Academie des Inscriptions if they wish to explore various properties of flints and stones in terms of magic and psychic powers. In the poem about stones attributed to Orpheus, these stones are divided into ophites and siderite, or "Snake Stone" and "Rock Star."

Sanchoniathon and Philo of Byblos, speaking about these "betylus," and call them "animated stones." Photius repeats what Damascena, Asclepiades, Isidor, and the physician Eusebius argued before. In particular, Eusebius never parted with his ophites, which he wore on his chest and from which he received the prophecy he heard "in a low voice that resembled a soft whistle." Of course, it's the same as the "quiet voice" Ilya heard at the entrance to the cave after the earthquake.[2]

This work contains several other examples of "talking stones."

The Old Testament gives us another account of "talking stones." God gave a gemstone breastplate to Aaron, the high priest of Israel, to help him spiritually discern the answers to people's questions that he asked God when praying in the tabernacle. Exodus 28:30 mentions mystical objects called the *Urim* and the *Thummim* (lights and perfections) that God instructed the Hebrew people to include in the breastplate: "Also put the Urim and the Thummim in the breastplate, so they may be over Aaron's heart whenever he enters the presence of the Lord. Thus Aaron will always bear the means of making decisions for the Israelites over his heart before the Lord." These stones, one white and the other black, would give a yes or no answer to a specific question.

Best-selling Russian author Vladimir Megre, describes Anastasia, a wise Siberian woman, who talks about her ancestral memory of the dolmens. Dolmens served as a bank for preserving knowledge of the human experience. Ancient keepers of vital knowledge for humanity deliberately locked themselves inside the dolmen, where they remained in a state of deep meditation, during which they transmitted vital knowledge to humanity. This information was picked up by those who served as channels, and also via clairaudience and automatic writing. Ancient keepers of vital knowledge sacrificed themselves in order to preserve ancient knowledge for future generations.[3] After the knowledge was preserved, only a pure soul could "talk to the stone" to access the special knowledge "locked" inside the dolmen. Maybe the human skeletons found inside some of the dolmens are the remains of the "knowledge transferrers"? Such dolmens even today are considered very powerful, and members of Anastasia's movement consider all North Caucasus dolmens to be sacred.

Flesh Eaters

In other parts of the world, ancient peoples built structures for possibly similar purposes of capturing one's soul. The "soul capture" of our ancestors inside the dolmen could explain the Egyptian sarcophagus in the Serapeum of Saqqara. Giant sarcophagi were built with heavy lids that one person could not lift. Sarcophagi were also found inside the pyramids in Egypt, with no human remains found in these sarcophagi or in the Serapeum as well, the same as inside most of the dolmens. A dolmen resembles a sarcophagus but with an entrance hole that is closed with a heavy plug. Some dolmens even have a distinctive sarcophagus shape (Figure 32). Could dolmens be built for the same purpose as the sarcophagi?

According to the ancient Egyptians, a sarcophagus was a ship on which the soul of the deceased floated away to the underworld. Another theory suggests that a sarcophagus was intended to help the soul separate from the physical body (which, although dead, continued to hold the soul). The soul was supposed to fly up to the court of Osiris (as described in the Egyptian *Book of the Dead*). The tradition of making a stone sarcophagus continues in some parts of the world (for example in Vietnam) to this day.

Another example of a sarcophagus acting as the "soul liberator" can be seen in the Mexican city of Palenque, where the "Temple of Inscriptions" contains the tomb of Pakal the Great. Palenque is known for its

Figure 32. Images of sarcophagus-like dolmens: dolmen Mirnuj 1 (Peaceful) by the river Tsuskhvadzh, left, and dolmen Chuhukt 4 in the Katkova gap, right.

archaeological complex consisting of several pyramids. Its most famous ruler was Lord Pakal, who, during his 68-year reign (the longest in the history of North and South America), created Palenque's most famous monuments. Pakal's sarcophagus has a large stone lid (Figure 33) that shows Pakal's soul leaving the body from his *dantian*, which, according to Taoists, is our "life force energy center."

I have one unforgettable memory associated with this stone lid from December 2012, when everyone was expecting the "end of the world." Radio and television were broadcasting the "exact time" remaining for the existence of a careless humanity and reflecting on the meaning of life. Despite this, having said good-bye

Figure 33. The stone lid of Pakal's sarcophagus.

to our parents and daughter, we flew to Palenque, Mexico. Not far from this place was "Monument 6"—the stele on which the prediction about the "end of the world" was engraved.

The media insisted that the Maya must be listened to, since they have achieved great success in astronomy and other sciences. The Maya invented chocolate and rubber, their own written language, effective agriculture, and irrigation canals; used the mathematical zero and fractions of a unit; created large cities and bridges without construction vehicles; and had flat roads and an accurate calendar.

The Maya, in fact, had two calendars: the 260-day tzolkin and the 365-day haab. The combination of the haab and tzolkin dates determined the exact date, which did not repeat again for 52 years. To denote the date in periods exceeding 52 years, the Maya used a "long count" calendar, which allowed them to uniquely determine the date and which did not repeat for 5,125 years. After this number of years, the calendar had to be "reset," so that the calendar would work again for the next 5,000-plus years.

As we already know, the world did not end in 2012. The stele indicated only that the "long count" of the Maya calendar (5,125 years) would soon be complete and that the calendar would begin anew. But no one wanted to delve into this, so everyone expected a catastrophe, or at least something extraordinary, at midnight on December 21, 2012, which happened to coincide with the winter solstice.

Back in December of 2012, the village of Palenque was full of free-spirited people and seekers of the unusual—young and old—dressed in bohemian clothes or as shamans and astrologers. Many of them stayed in Mayan villages, where residents gave them a "corner," since all the hotels had been reserved for a year (villages like Palenque have no large "all-inclusive" tourist hotels). Local restaurants worked around the clock and we were enjoying freshly baked flat cakes with cheese (*quesadia*), hand-pressed orange juice, and other Mexican delicacies.

Standing in one of the lines for tortillas, we talked with a bohemian-looking woman, who told me that the previous night she had been in the crypt of King Pakal, where a shaman was conducting a ritual. That was incredible! I knew that the crypt was under the protection of UNESCO, and archaeologists have long banned tourists to it. This is due to the belief that moisture from human breathing can affect the atmosphere in the crypt and damage the delicate coloring of the sarcophagus. Not even heads of state visiting the monument were allowed to look at the "holy of holies," the famous cover of the sarcophagus of Pakal. What about a whole group of people, breathing and fumigating the room with herbs during a ritual?

She said that if we wanted to participate in the ritual, we must find a shaman who can take people there. The shaman then decides whether we are worthy of this honor—he will not take money, and if he says no, he cannot be persuaded.

We immediately went to the Mayan village where this shaman lived so we could be "tested" for the possibility of visiting the crypt. Unfortunately, we did not find the shaman there. "I guess he felt like we did not fit in and decided not to waste time meeting with us," I jokingly said with a sad smile. There was only one night left until the "end of the world."

Back at the hotel, a nondescript little man approached us and said in Spanish, "I heard you want to visit the tomb of Pakal? I can arrange it for $500 US dollars." He did not want to bargain, explaining that he must share this money with many other "organizers."

After a brief discussion, we decided that the end of the world was coming soon, and who knows what would happen, so we agreed. The "guide" said that we had to wear dark clothes and hiking boots. He would come at 11 p.m. "And do not tell anyone where you're going," he added.

Eleven o'clock sharp he came to take us for the trip. We had already visited the complex that afternoon and had some idea where we were going. The car stopped about 2 km (1.2 miles) kilometers before the gate, where we had previously bought tickets. "Then we go on foot. Do not use flashlights," he commanded. We went through the jungle. Some animals howled in the distance and we heard noises in the bushes, but we could not use our flashlight and could only stare at the barely visible silhouette of the guide, who was walking briskly ahead. Approaching the fence of the archaeological complex, he stopped and whistled softly. Suddenly, from behind the bushes appeared a dark-skinned man dressed in all black with a submachine gun over his shoulder. They exchanged something in silence and the armed man disappeared in the dark. We met silent armed men guarding the archaeological complex several more times on the way to the crypt.

"Climb the pyramid and go up. Find the passage covered with boards. See that you would not be visible when the moon rises," he ordered. Since it was impossible to use a flashlight, we hardly saw what was under our feet and jumped from one step to another, risking breaking our legs or, worse, our necks.

The night was quiet and without a single light. At the top, I looked at the huge stars above my head and at the outlines of the pyramid barely visible in the darkness. I thought that the Maya probably saw them like that many centuries ago.

The guide gave us a flashlight, saying that now we could use it, and closed the door of the tomb behind him. We remained completely alone in the middle of the night inside a huge pyramid and in a tightly closed crypt. It was very quiet.

I read in a tourist guide that although archaeologists have previously explored the pyramids of Palenque, Pakal's crypt was not immediately found, as it was artfully disguised under tons of rubble. It took four years to clean the rubble from the stairs leading to the crypt and, in the end, archaeologists had to dig up the sarcophagus. The crypt had not been looted and Pakal's remains were still in the coffin. When they opened the sarcophagus, they saw that Pakal's face was covered with a jade mask and heavy necklaces of beads hung around his neck. The crypt was surrounded by sculptures and molded bas-reliefs depicting the ascension of this supreme ruler to God. Traces of paint showed that all of the sculptures were once beautifully painted, which was common for many Mayan sculptures of the time.

I remembered that during his lifetime Pakal was famous for being able to communicate with the spirits of the dead. *Can the spirit of Pakal talk with the living?*, I thought. But the skeleton, along with the ornaments, had long since been taken to the National Museum of Anthropology in Mexico. Perhaps the spirit of Pakal is now roaming there. We spent about an hour near the sarcophagus, the famous plate glowing white in the depths. Researchers of ancient astronauts such as Erich von Däniken argue that the lid depicts Maya, who controls the spacecraft. He sits in a special chair, a breathing device attached to his nose, and holds the handle of the wheel. We looked at the lid of the sarcophagus and thought about of our own explanation of that scene. It seemed to me that the stone plate with Maya in the spacecraft trembled a little, like a rocket ready to take off. "Have a good trip!" I said to him. There is a theory that the "real" Maya flew to another planet or even to another galaxy.

It was an unforgettable night! We missed the end of the world, as we were in the crypt at midnight and did not check our watches. I do not regret the money that I paid for the trip, as it was worth it.

In the morning, we visited the archaeological complex again. The day after the failed end of the world was gloomy, with a fine drizzling rain, as if nature herself was disappointed that nothing much happened. The world continued to go on, people walked along the paths (climbing the pyramids is strictly prohibited), meditated, and took selfies. Everyone was solemn, and few people laughed or spoke loudly. Humanity had survived yet another predicted "doomsday."

I looked at people's faces and thought that I did not want to witness the real end of the world, no matter how "interesting" it could have been. Besides, to whom could I tell it to later?! Whether the end of the world will happen or not depends only on us, on all humanity. I hope that it never comes.

The sarcophagus tradition can also be traced in other ancient megalithic structures, for example, in the Plain of Jars in Laos (Figure 34). Each jar is a monolith with an entrance that is tightly locked with a

Figure 34. Left, Plain of Jars, Laos; right, a jar with the lid.

heavy stone lid—the same principal as in the sarcophagus or dolmens. In some jars archaeologists found human skeletons.

In North Caucasus, each dolmen's hole was tightly closed with a heavy stone plug. Because some dolmens contained human remains in the fetal position, we may think that the ancients believed that the soul must leave the body in the same position as it came in at the time of birth. After the flesh was completely disintegrated, "liberating" the soul, the plug was removed and the soul was allowed to leave. There was no need to move a very heavy lid for this. The use of a plug was an "improved" technology in comparison to the "standard" way a sarcophagus's lid was removed. Could it be that the dolmens were built just for this purpose—to be used as a sarcophagus? In my opinion, the purpose of dolmens was much larger, as we will see later in the book.

Asian Connection

The front blocks of several dolmens have bas-reliefs of a stylized dolmen or other structure with a similar shape (Figure 35).

These images are reminiscent of the Indian *toran*, a structure associated with the Buddhist *stupa*, or even the Japanese *torii* gate that is a symbol of the Shinto religion (Figure 36). The function of torans and toriis is to mark the entrance to a sacred space. When you go under these gates you are spiritually cleansed. Maybe because of the rectangular shape, dolmens were also used for sacred cleansing?

Figure 35. Dolmens with an image of a symmetrically rectangular shape.

Figure 36. Typical Buddhist toran in India, left, and a Japanese Shinto torii, right.

Figure 37. A hokora, or kami shrine, used in the Shinto religion.

Figure 38. Dolmen "Klady 3" in Adygea (from the Klady "Treasure" tract) with a rectangular entrance.

Shinto gods, or *kami*, are sacred spirits that take the form of things and concepts important to life, such as wind, rain, mountains, trees, rivers, and fertility. Shinto shrines dedicated to kami are called *hokora* and resemble dolmens (Figure 37).

Dolmens in Japan and India have rectangular entrances and, interestingly, several Caucasus dolmens have rectangular entrances as well (Figure 38). These dolmens look similar to the Shinto hokora.

Interestingly, heaven (*tian*) in Chinese ancient beliefs is round and the earth (*di*) is square. The two words together (*tiandi*) mean "everything, the universe." This belief can be seen in ancient and modern Asian constructions and artifacts (Figure 39). Also, ancient Chinese coins were also round with a square hole in the middle.

According to fêng shui, a Chinese philosophical system that teaches principles for harmonizing human health and prosperity with the surrounding environment as well as enhancing the flow of universal energy, the building has to face water and be protected by mountains behind and across from it.

Figure 39. Dolmen-like ironwork.

This philosophy crept into European architecture in the form of oeil-de-boeuf ("eye of an ox" in French). This is a small oval or round window put in an upper story or on a roof (Figure 40, left). Windows in this style were common in baroque France.

Holes in buildings are common in Asia, for example, buildings in Hong Kong are constructed with square holes called "dragon holes" (Figure 40, right). Hong Kong legends tell of dragons that live in the mountains and hold positive and powerful energy. This energy flows through buildings as the dragons go from the mountains to the water to drink and bathe. Blocking this energy is thought to bring misfortune.

Figure 40. Oeil-de-boeuf element, left, and "dragon holes" in buildings in Hong Kong, right.

Dolmens are also built near water and among mountains. They also have holes for flowing positive energy. Is it just a coincidence that a rectangular shape was chiseled on dolmens or is there a strong connection to the Buddhist and Shinto religions?

Indian Connection

According to some researchers, dolmen builders were proto-Aryans who arrived in the Caucasus from Central Europe.[4] Archaeologist Leo Klejn indicates that dolmen culture has specific Indo-Aryan characteristics.[5] These proto-Aryan tribes were Hattians, who played a huge role in the formation of the Circassian and Abkhazian cultures, along with the Kaskians, whom many authoritative scholars consider among the ancestors of the Abkhaz-Adyghe (Circassians). Numerous items of material culture and the similarities in their languages, way of life, traditions, customs, religious beliefs, toponymics, and many other things attest to the close relationship between the Hattians, Kaskians, and Abkhaz-Adyghe.

Hattians had close contact with Mesopotamia, Syria, and ancient Greece. Thus, the Hattian culture preserved a rich heritage derived from the traditions of the ancient ethnoses of Anatolia, in addition to borrowing from the cultures of Mesopotamia, Syria, and the Caucasus, especially the Abkhaz-Adyghe. One of the irrefutable proofs that Hattians and

Abkhaz-Adyghe are related can be seen in the area of toponymy. In the region of Trabzon (in modern Turkey) and further northwest along the Black Sea coast, many modern researchers (for example I. Dunaevskaya[6]) have noted a number of ancient and modern names of localities, rivers, ravines, etc., that the ancestors of the Abkhaz-Adyghe left.

The Hattians also had significant influence on the mighty Hittite kingdom in the second millennium BC. The Hittites, mentioned several times in the Bible, were an Indo-European people of the Bronze Age who lived in Asia Minor, where they founded the Hittite kingdom centered on Hattusa. Moving later to India, they brought with them the cult of their gods. Several ancient Hittite tables have interesting dolmen-like figures and four round bumps, as can be found on some dolmens. We will discuss these bumps later in the book (Figure 41).

The proto-Indian peoples are sometimes known as Aryans. According to the Vedas, the god of fertility for the Aryans was the god Rudra, later known as Shiva. In many Hindu temples, the god Shiva appears inside of an oval cavern in a dolmen-like structure in a column. This iconic representation of Shiva illustrates the legend of Lingodbhava ("emergence of the Linga") and is found in various puranas, the ancient tales of India. Linga means the "form" and represents energy and strength. This column is sometimes called the "axis mundi" or the pillar at the center of the world, cracking the surface of the earth and splitting the sky. The column in Lingodbhava represents a huge column of fire (Light Linga) that split the earth and blazed up through the sky to pierce the highest heavens.

Figure 41. Ancient Hittite table with dolmen-like figure and bumps.

The tale goes that once the deities Vishnu and Brahma contested for superiority, and to show them the futility of their battle, Shiva took the form of the Great Universal Fire (the Great Linga) and asked Brahma and Vishnu to measure this fire.

Brahma and Vishnu stopped arguing and decided to find the beginning and end of the Great Linga. Vishnu took the form of a boar, Varaha Dev, the third avatar of Lord Vishnu, and descended into the earth, while Brahma took the form of a swan, Khans, and flew up into the sky. However, neither Vishnu nor Brahma could find the summits and foundations of this great all-encompassing fire. This made them realize that there is someone greater. After that, in perfect humility, they started worshiping the great pillar of fire.

Satisfied with their worship, Shiva appeared on Linga's body with a thousand hands and feet, and with the sun, moon, and fire as his three eyes. Then Shiva told Brahma and Vishnu that they support his left and right sides accordingly, and that their separation into three is an illusion; in reality they are only one. From that time, Linga became the object of universal worship. In commemoration of this great phenomenon, the iconographic image of Linga appeared in the form of the Lingodbhava that sealed this event. In most cases, this column appears inside of a dolmen-like structure (Figure 42).

The Hindu scriptures also report five more forms of lingas. These lingas represent the earth, water, fire, air (wind) and sky (or ether).

We can see these five forms in the association with dolmens:

- **Earth:** The dolmen's rectangular base is rooted to the earth. Stones that are used for dolmens are from the "womb" of the earth.
- **Water:** There is always a water source near a dolmen.
- **Air (wind):** Dolmens are built on mountains, where wind is more noticeable.
- **Fire:** The orientation of dolmens on the terrain as a rule fits into the arc of sunrise and sunset, representing the sacred fire, the sun.
- **Sky (ether, space):** Dolmens are located on the mountains, the closest distance to the sky.

These five elements correspond with the human senses:

- **Fire:** We see it (sight).
- **Water:** We hear it (hearing).
- **Earth:** We smell and taste it (smell and taste).

- **Air:** We feel air movement and wind on our skin (touch).
- **Space (ether):** We have a sense of balance and position in space, acceleration, a sense of weight (the vestibular apparatus).

These five elements exist in other philosophical systems and religions, for example, in Buddhism and the Chinese Wu Xing.

An important feature of the Hindu temple is its square base. This form was always conceived as rooted to the earth and, hence, had to be built with the most durable material for construction, namely, stone.[7]

Linga (Figure 42) is an iconic representation of the god Shiva and by nature is a "crossing place" where the worlds are interconnected. The linga is often represented as resting on *yoni*, a stylized representation of female genitalia representing the Hindu goddess Shakti.[8] In Hindu philosophy, according to tantra, yoni is the origin of life.[9]

Figure 42. Airavatesvara Temple at Darasuram, 12th century AD, left; a linga, right.

Caucasus dolmens also have a hole (iconic representation of female genitalia) that is plugged with a phallic-like lid (iconic representation of the male genitalia). Could it be that dolmens were earlier representations of Hattian worship of the origin of life and its generative power? What if it was later transformed into worshiping the god Shiva? Maybe the mysterious dolmen builders were Hattians whose beliefs influenced Indian religion?

Greek Connection

After the fall of the Hittites around 1200 BC, the Greek civilization began to flourish in Anatolia (Asia Minor), which is bounded by the Black Sea to the north. The Nephilim (the sons of God) were biblical giants who emerged from the Caucasus Mountains, and in ancient Greek mythology, the Titans (the Nephilim) were giants who where revered as gods.

According to Greek mythology, one of the Titans, Prometheus (meaning "forethoughtful" in Greek) was mankind's greatest benefactor. He taught mankind about mathematics, writing, medicine, astronomy, fortune-telling, magic, and how to construct stone houses, chariots and sails. He gave the human race fire and the skill of metalwork.

When Zeus decreed that man must present a portion of each animal they sacrificed to the gods, Prometheus decided to trick Zeus and help man. He created two piles to use in the sacrificial process, one with the bones wrapped in fat and the other with the good meat hidden in the hide. He then bade Zeus to pick, and Zeus picked the bones. From then on, humans would keep meat for themselves and burn the bones wrapped in fat as an offering to the gods.

In his anger over the trick, Zeus took fire away from mankind. However, Prometheus lit a torch from the sun and brought it back to man. Zeus was enraged that man again had fire and he decided to inflict a terrible punishment on both man and Prometheus. Prometheus, in eternal punishment, must pass countless ages riveted to a crag on the shores of the ocean in the trackless waste of Scythia (the name the ancient Greeks gave to all the lands northeast of Europe and the northern coast of the Black Sea):

> ...and those who dwell in the land of Colchis, the maidens fearless in fight; and the Scythian multitude that inhabits the most remote region of the earth bordering the Maeotian lake; and the warlike flower of Arabia, which hold the high-cragged citadel near the Caucasus, a hostile host that roars among the sharp-pointed spears.[10]

To punish man for Prometheus's help, Zeus had his son Hephaestus create a mortal of stunning beauty: Pandora, the first woman. The gods gave Pandora many gifts of wealth, but Zeus then had his son Hermes give her a deceptive heart and a lying tongue. A final gift was a jar, which Pandora was forbidden to open. Thus completed, Zeus sent Pandora down to Epimetheus, a Titan who was staying among the men.

If you look at the map of the Caucasian coast, "the most remote region of the earth" includes the waters of the Maeotian lake (the Azov Sea today), the Taman Peninsula and the Kerch Strait, and Colchis, the ancient territory just south of the current-day Russian cities of Sochi and Tuapse—where many dolmens exist.

What kind of cosmic energy was the "fire of Prometheus" that was taken from the sun (space)? Interestingly, in 2003, NASA started a new project, Project Prometheus, to develop nuclear-powered systems for long-duration space missions. Nevertheless, this energy was associated with the area where thousands of dolmens later stood.

The energy given as a gift to humans (the solar energy in the form of fire) was obviously a "good" energy for humans. Was it a "bad" energy (in the form of Pandora's box) that Zeus decided to punish man with? Why did Aeschylus start the verse that describes the punishment of Prometheus with the following sentence: "Now the whole earth cries aloud in lamentation"?[11] Was it because of man's grief for Prometheus's punishment by Zeus, or because of Zeus's revenge on humankind?

If we think about this myth, we can recall the earlier discussion about dolmens emitting electromagnetic waves. Abundant research has confirmed that dolmens generate high-frequency vibrations and electromagnetic waves. The stones with which the dolmens were built include quartz crystals that can convert mechanical energy into electrical energy and vice versa. Due to tectonic block movement, earthquakes, and the tidal influences of the sun, moon, and other planets, the quartz in the dolmen stones creates acoustic and electrical waves.

Maybe the dolmen plug was used as a special activation device that "switched on" or "switched off" a dolmen (by changing the intensity of the electromagnetic field), similar to the golem of Jewish folklore who was activated by the special word *shem* written on a piece of paper and inserted in the golem's mouth or forehead.[12]

Dolmens were also built in cavities in the earth's crust, where strong energy flows are observed. The quartz crystals are then charged with power according to the size of the corresponding stone plate. The dolmen's inner camera acts as a resonator that, due to its parallel walls, emits a standing energy wave through the entrance hole in the dolmen's front plate; sometimes a plasmoid body is even formed. These energy fluctuations increase according to the number of dolmens "connected together" to form a single system. This may affect the weather and biological processes in the area of the dolmens, accelerating or decreasing the growth of microorganisms, affecting plants and animals, as well as influencing human behavior and health. This will be discussed later in the book.

What if dolmens were built to use this power, either to absorb the "good" energy (gift to humans according to the Greek mythology) or dissipate the "bad" energy (punishment by gods according to the ancient Greeks)? Dolmens could have been built for the purpose of "healing" the area and removing the negative energy in order to allow the nature and people to be unharmed.

Olmec and Mayan Connection

During a visit to the Parque-Museo La Venta in Villahermosa, Mexico, I saw familiar images of dolmens (Figure 43). The museum had many dolmen monuments that belonged to the Olmec civilization, an ancient Mexican civilization of which we know very little. Just as with the Caucasus dolmens, there is no writing on the structures that can explain the purpose of their "typical" dolmen. The Mayas, Zapotecs, Toltecs, and Aztecs were among the Mesoamericans who inherited and built upon the Olmec traditions, and several such dolmens were discovered in the area. Therefore, we can learn about this monument by studying the Maya.

Figure 43. Dolmen in Mexico. This ancient monument belongs to the Olmec civilization of early Mexico.

In Altar 4 from La Venta (Figure 44), the front of the monument displays a round "door" to the "dolmen," which is framed with some kind of rays, as if energy is flowing from the inside out (or right into) the dolmen.

A creature inside the dolmen wears a "bat hat." In Mayan mythology (and probably in Olmec), Camazotz was a bat god who feeds on blood and was associated with night, death, and sacrifice. The bat was considered to be a creature coming from the dark worlds. Recall any legend where a bat appears—for example, vampires—and it looks like bats were always associated with dark, negative energy.

The Mayan tradition has a dolmen-like structure known as *xanil nah* (Figure 45), which represents the place where Mayans come from. Mayans believe they came from a place called *Pa Tulan* or *Pa Civan* (the Mayan word *pa* means "place"), where *sipapu*, the tunnel between the worlds, was located. It links the stars and planets as well as the world

Figure 44. Altar 4 from La Venta, Mexico.

eras, so that when one era ends and another begins, the sipapu shows the way.[13]

Mayans also refer to this place as a cave, the entrance of which was guarded by a bat. The bat was a kind of mediator between the world of the living and the world of the dead. In the Mayan tradition, their ancestors once managed to get out of the underworld and settle on living land.

In South America, we can find other places associated with a passage or doorway to

Figure 45. Typical dolmen-like stone effigy in Mayan structures, in Labna, Mexico. Note the round hole at the end of the front wall.

another world, for example, a megalithic door in Peru called the "Devil's Doorway" is known from legend as "a doorway to the land of the gods" (Figure 46).

Figure 46. The Devil's Doorway in Peru.

This legend talks about great heroes who passed through this door to a glorious new life of immortality in the Otherworld. The modern name, Devil's Doorway, came from Catholics after the conquest. Locals often report blue light emanating from a tunnel inside the rock, or

Figure 47. Door to the Otherworld located in Yazilikaya in modern-day Turkey.

strange people dressed in unusual clothing emerging from it and traveling toward Lake Titicaca. Such doors are not unknown. Another similar door is in Yazilikaya, Turkey (Figure 47).

Historians insist that America became known to the rest of the world only after Columbus "discovered" it and that ancient peoples did not travel to other continents. However, much evidence says the opposite. In their own words, Mayan people say they came from the north. What if they used to live in the Caucasus area and built dolmens as a "cave" symbol, that is, the entrance to the underworld from where they came from. Some researchers have found similarities between Mayan and several North Caucasus languages.[14] In my opinion, Mayan "dolmen" monuments and North Caucasus dolmens look very similar.

Sun Worshippers

The central role of the sun for all living things on earth was probably observed in very ancient times. In all religions, myths, and fairy tales around the world, the sun occupies a central place. All peoples considered the sun the main deity, from the radiant god Helios of the ancient Greeks, and Dazhbog and Yarilo from the ancient Slavs, to Inti from the Incas in South America.

Sun worship is often seen as primitive but is, in fact, a sophisticated awe-inspiring system of worship that appeals to the senses and captivates the mind with its elaborate ceremonies. This system of worship has been perpetuated throughout the generations, and in our time forms the basis of earth religions, Buddhism, Hinduism, and Catholicism. In the mysteries of Catholicism, sun worship reaches its highest form. The names of the gods have changed, but the system of worship is the same.

Certain characteristics distinguish temples for sun worship:[15]

- Orientation to the south-north and east-west
- Incorporation of concentric circles and solar symbols into the design
- Presence of water nearby

Interestingly, we can find all of the above characteristics in dolmen orientation and construction. We can even find typical solar symbols on some dolmens.

The facades of the North Caucasus dolmens mainly face south (south-north orientation)—333 of 644 dolmens studied—and 152 dolmens face east (east-west orientation). A small number, 93, face southeast, and 21 face southwest. Only 45 dolmens are oriented differently. V. Markovin, who studied these monuments, concluded that such orientation was not accidental and does not depend on the "terrain configuration."[16] And as we have already shown, there is always a source of water near the dolmens (Figures 48 and 49).

Figure 48. Concentric circles representing the sun on a dolmen on the Archiz River, left; sun symbol on a dolmen in Lazarevsky City District, right.

Together with spirals, concentric circles are some of the most common icons of ancient art and are also associated with the concept of *axis mundi*. That is, the abode of the motionless sun, and its pedestal is identified as the cosmic center, or the connection between heaven and earth. Atlanteans supposedly had concentric rings of water channels alternating with those of Earth.

The sun cross symbol is also associated with the wheel of the chariot of the sun god.[17] Many archaeologists embrace the sun cross theory and it is widely accepted due to an interest in finding a pre-Christian origin for the symbol of Christianity. The disc of the sun was regarded as a wheel, hence, the myth that the sun god drives in a chariot across the

Figure 49. Examples of sun symbols on dolmen plugs.

heavens. The same symbol, a cross inside of a circle, was found in burial mounds throughout North and South America.[18]

As for the vast number of dolmens that have been built, we may not know the reason. However, the main characteristics of sun-worshiping structures are definitely present. Could it be that a sun-worshiping culture built the North Caucasus dolmens?

Dolmens and Archeoastronomy

Archeoastronomy is the study of how ancient peoples understood the sky, how they used this knowledge, what role the sky played, and how it influenced their cultures. This study has already been done for other megaliths. For example, Gerald S. Hawkins and John B. White in their book, *Stonehenge Decoded*, suggested that Stonehenge is not only an ancient sanctuary but also an observatory, precisely marking the set, astronomically significant directions of the sun, moon, and stars. The builders of megalithic structures "embedded" in many monuments such astronomically significant dates, such as the solstices and equinoxes.

This is typical for many North Caucasus dolmens as well. According to Mikhail Kudin in his article "Dolmens and Ritual," the connection between dolmens and archeoastronomy was first studied by M. K. Teshev,[19] an employee of the Tuapse Local Lore and History Museum. For a long time, this archeoastronomy aspect with dolmens also involved geologist V. M. Kondryakov.[20] According to Kudin, one dolmen that

Figure 50. Pyramid-shaped dolmen in Mamed Canyon on the Kuapse River.

was built with a definitive astronomical purpose is the pyramid-shaped dolmen in Mamed Canyon, located on the Kuapse River, which was carved in a huge rock of dark gray sandstone (Figure 50).

The width of the rock is more than 5 m (16.4 ft.) and the length is 8 m (26.2 ft.). Most of the rock surface was left untreated, but the dolmen is carved so that the west side of the rock is the shape of a pyramid. The top of this pyramid accurately indicates the point of sunrise over the ridge at the equinoxes, March 22 and September 21 (Figure 50, left).

The top of this pyramid is cut in such a way that the first ray of the sun at the equinoxes appears on the verge of the top and a full disc "seats" in the center. The first rays of the sun run along the edge of the pyramid and fall into the center of the overlap of the dolmen. As Kudin explains, the facade of this dolmen and its aperture are directed to the south (the azimuth is 180 degrees) marking the sunset at the winter solstice. Unfortunately, the overlap did not survive. Even in 1907, when A. Miller[21] first described this dolmen, the overlapping was missing.

The dolmen represents the bosom of the mother goddess, who carries a divine child in its womb for nine months, until the winter solstice, when the "old" sun is dying out.[22] Later, the "young" sun is born from the "belly" of the dolmen, and then every day the sun rises higher and higher in the sky[23]. Many gods were born on the day of the winter solstice, such as the Roman sun god Saturn. Thus some researchers suggest that the burial in a dolmen was connected with the fertile power of the goddess's womb and revived with the sun. Also, the symbol of the pyramid with an all-seeing eye on top is well known in many religious and occult traditions, such as Freemasonry.

We have briefly touched on the connection between the orientation of dolmens and the significance to the calendar and astronomy. One can assume that almost all dolmens, even oriented to the north, have astronomical significance, marking the direction of certain stars and constellations. These assumptions are, of course, quite controversial and require further detailed investigation, but that megalith builders oriented many dolmens with such astronomically significant dates like the solstices and equinoxes is pretty obvious.

Dolmens and the Paleolithic Calendar

With methods of paleoastronomy, we can reconstruct the concepts of space and time, life and death, astral mythology, and other important aspects of the spiritual life of the ancient people who built dolmens for purposes known only to them and which remain a mystery.

The previous section discussed dolmens as marking the solstices and equinoxes. Some dolmens marked sunrises and moonsets as well. The dolmen builders certainly paid a lot of attention to the moon, especially since the direction of the moonrise and moonset largely coincide with sunrises and sunsets. During the 28 days of her cycle over a year, the moon moves over the horizon just like the sun.

M. Kudin, in his article "Calendar Motives in Dolmen Culture," studied ornamental motifs on the walls of the Caucasian dolmens, and he suggested that the geometrical ornamentation on a dolmen on the Zhane River is an ancient calendar (Figure 51). He argued that zigzag patterns on the walls of this dolmen can be called rhythmic, as they reflect the natural rhythms of day and night, the seasons, the growing and waning moon, and the rhythm of the cosmos. The triangles on the front and side walls represent months of the year, periods of growth, and the waning moon. The growing and flowing lines are similar to the phases of the moon, and the vertices of triangles indicate the full moon.

Figure 51. Zigzag patterns on the walls of a dolmen on the Zhane River.

The direction of the triangles pointing downward may reflect an ancient female symbol of the moon goddess.

Kudin also pointed out that understanding the ancient calendars may be difficult and may not make sense to readers unfamiliar with astronomy. It is for this reason that many modern historians believe that ancient peoples did not have the highest astronomical and calendar knowledge. Other researchers praise the perfection of ancient calendars as something amazing.

The people who lived in ancient times turned their gaze to the sky every day. The sky was a clock, a compass, and a calendar. But today we have our watches, compasses, and calendars, and we no longer get practical information from the sky. The starry sky—the moon, sun, and stars—is known today perhaps only to astronomy experts.

The astronomical orientation of the dolmen facades, including their calendar cycle designs, should not lead us to conclude that the dolmen is only an observatory or calendar. The purpose of these ancient monuments is multifaceted. Each dolmen is *imago mundi*, an "image of the world." The reflection of celestial phenomena in the dolmens shows the desire of ancient people to participate in the holy law of death and rebirth that played out in the sky over their heads.

There are many debunkers of the theory that megaliths were built for the purpose of observing special calendar dates, such as the start of the agricultural or hunting season, for simple, practical reasons. Not all dolmens face west, so why go to such lengths to build impressive and time-consuming megaliths when a simple, strategically placed marker could indicate the same events as the solstice and equinox?

Just noticing a natural marker could suffice. Often, several important astronomical phenomena are observed from the facade of the monument. M. Teshev wrote that "In the days of the solstices and equinoxes, sunrise and sunset as well as the moon (at high and low positions) astonishingly coincide with some high peaks or gorges in the surrounding valley of the mountains and ridges."[24]

In my opinion, Caucasus dolmens were not built simply to act as mere calendars but were erected for more complex purposes and served more than one goal. However, we may never discover what that goal was.

Progress-Boosting Technology and Baby-Making Machine

Many authors have noted that dolmens, like megaliths in other parts of the world, are located on tectonic anomalies of the earth's crust. Visually, the crustal faults are valleys and floodplains of rivers that resulted from the destruction of the mountain massif in fault zones (Figure 52).

In 2005, the Krasnodar Regional Office of the Euro-Asian Geophysical Society confirmed research indicating that the axes of convergent, seismically active zones of immersion of tectonic plates go through areas where dolmens exist.[26] The theory that their location is perhaps connected with the crustal faults, and biologically affects people, was expressed in 1992 by Soviet scientists R. Furdui and U. Shvardak in their work "The Charm of Mystery."[27]

First we have to define the geological terms *lineament* and *fault*. A fault is a crack in the earth's crust. Typically, faults are associated with, or form, the boundaries between the earth's *tectonic plates*. The earth's crust consists of 15 to 20 moving tectonic plates. The plates can be thought of as pieces of a cracked shell that rest on the hot, molten rock of the earth's mantle and fit neatly against one another. The heat from radioactive processes within the planet's interior causes the plates

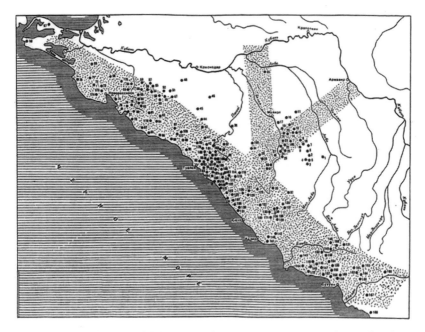

Figure 52. Distribution of dolmens in the Western Caucasus. The circles show dolmens and dolmen groups; gray shading shows the lineament zones.[25]

to move, sometimes toward and sometimes away from each other. This movement is called "plate motion," or "tectonic shift." A *lineament* is a liner feature on the earth's surface, such as a fault. Typically, a lineament will include a fault-aligned valley, a series of fault- or fold-aligned hills, a straight coastline, or a combination of all these features.

Territory in the Russian Federation is located in seismically active regions and is generally characterized by moderate *seismicity* (the occurrence or frequency of earthquakes). The exception is the region of the Northern Caucasus, which is characterized by the highest seismicity in the European part of Russia.

Searching in 1995 for the reason why no dolmens exist in the coastal area between the settlement of Dagomys and the Abkhazian River Khashupse, archaeologists N. Kondryakov, together with his father, V. Kondryakov, found that all dolmens stand in places of tectonic disturbances.[28] Because this area suffered no significant tectonic disturbances, dolmens were not built there. How ancient people were able to identify these disturbances (energy) is another question.

Several researchers, among them A. Fedorov, argue about the influence of unknown geological factors, such as geological faults, seismicity, geomagnetic fields, and solar activity, on various types of human activity. In his work "The Influence of Geotectonics on the Activity of the Caucasus Population," he states that people living in such areas are affected by some unknown factor, and that social phenomena are largely determined by any geological activity (Figure 53).[29]

Numbers on the left: (1) barrows (*kurgans*); (2) settlement of Yasenov Polyana; (3) mounds near the village of Novosvobodnaya and dolmen field (more than 300 dolmens); (4) treasure near the village of Staromyshastovskaya, Scythian monuments; (5) barrows near the village of Kellermesskaya; (6) Uly burial mounds; (7) barrows near the village of Kostromskaya, megalithic monuments 3000 BC; (8) megalithic complex Psynako 1; (9) *top star*, dolmen field near the village of Kamennomostsky (Khadzhokh) (about 280 monuments); (10) *bottom star*, dolmen field near the village of Dakhovskaya (more than 200 buildings); (11) dolmen field near the village of Bagovskaya.

A significant number of studies have demonstrated that seismicity affects the activity of the population in the respective regions. Fedorov points out that all areas of increased dolmen concentration are located in major lineament zones—in the Taman-Absheron mega-lineament zone and in the Sochi-Stavropol lineament zone (Figures 52 and 53). All dolmens are located along local faults at the nodes where these faults intersect, and all cultures after the "dolmen culture" developed around these areas of dolmen concentration (Figure 53). The point is that ancient megalith builders put their monuments in these areas of intensive geological activity.

The emergence of these cultures, and the most important religious and political centers belonging to these cultures, appeared to have occurred under the influence of an unknown geological factor, according to Feodorov, with high seismicity leading to certain

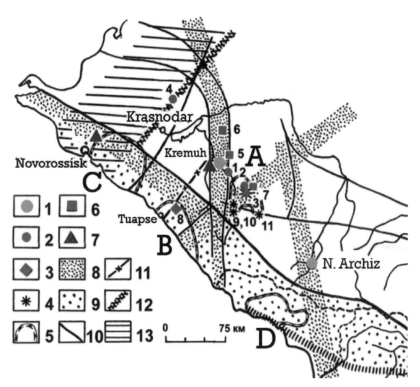

Figure 53. The most important archaeological sites of the North Caucasus. (1) political and religious centers; (2) the important archaeological monuments of the Maykop culture; (3) the megalithic complex at Psynako 1; (4) dolmens fields; (5) areas of increased concentration of dolmens (denoted by the letters A, B, C, D); (6) the most important Scythian archaeological monuments; (7) the location where the Adyghe tribes started; (8) lineament zones available on the cosmotectonic map; (9) Taman-Absheron mega-lineament zone; (10) long lineaments/faults available on the map seen from space; (11) the fault that is marked on the maps; (12) Athenian-Catherine (Afino-Ecaterininskiy) deep fault; (13) Novorossiysk-Manych linear zone.[30]

changes in thinking and perception. Presumably, these same factors can explain a number of the mental effects observed in and around the dolmens.

I think that this "unknown factor" is the influence of the megaliths, in this case the dolmens. Dolmens amplify energy that emanates from tectonic plates that move due to the tidal actions of the moon and the sun, along with frequent small earthquakes that shake the quartz-enriched dolmen blocks.

Scientists such as G. Chernyavsky and B. Skrebushevsky have noticed the following anomalies, which are among the most important dynamic precursors of earthquakes in the area of the dolmens:

- Increase in the low-frequency radiation flux
- Increase in microwaves (super high-frequency radiation, or SHF radiation) and extremely high frequency (EHF) radiation
- Abnormal changes in the polarization of the electromagnetic field (EMF) of the earth's rising radiation
- Anomalies in the atmospheric electric field above the earthquake source as well as in the magnetically conjugate regions of the ionosphere (which has recently been proposed for predicting earthquakes)[31]

It is also known that the capitals of the most powerful and stable states in the region arose and existed at the areas of most tectonic activity, around 44 degrees east longitude. This is where we find both the largest concentration of dolmens and areas that lead in historical and political development.

Based on a large body of data, Fedorov showed that cultures that formed in this area were known for the higher political, military, artistic, social, scientific, and risk-taking abilities required for establishing a strong civilization with continued progress.[32] He concluded that increased seismicity and the influence of tectonic activity caused by unknown geological factors led to certain changes in the mental state of the population in the regions and contributed to the formation of an appropriate system of values and culture in general—both behavioral and socio-political—ensuring the survival of the human community in these conditions. The main element of this type of culture is strength—both in the proper sense of the word (violence) and in the force of customs (prohibitions), traditions, and laws (coercion).

Fedorov also noted the area's negative effect. The fault zones (lineaments) displayed an increase in morbidity, mortality, accident rate, and

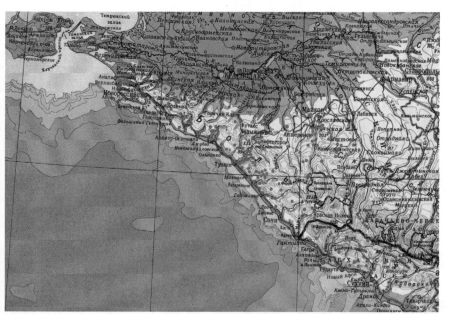

Map of the dolmens of the Krasnodar Krai. Red dots indicate groups of dolmens.

A typical dolmen in the Gelendzhik area (Pshada village).

Dolmen with a "false" plug, Tuapse area.

Dolmen with decorative geometric patterns and bas-reliefs in the village of Vozrozhdenie on the Janet River.

Dolmen in the Gelendzhik region of Russia with bas-relief and round projections.

Example of a pattern on a dolmen near Lazarevsky City District. *Inset,* closeup of the fragment.

Dolmen with polygonal masonry. The Leso-Kyafar area of the Karachay-Cherkess Republic.

tendency toward violence. Maybe this is because the dolmens, after a long time of neglect and lack of maintenance, are now out of tune?

At the same time, by the end of the 20th century, Russian scientists had accumulated a large body of data on the neurophysiological effects of the electromagnetic field, prolonged nonionizing radiation, oscillations, and other anomalies of the geomagnetic field on brain biochemistry, the central nervous system, behavioral responses, suggestibility levels, and purposeful mental activity. Thus, for example, mental illnesses in the area of the Kursk magnetic anomaly are 120 to 160 percent higher than in regions where EMF anomalies are absent; rates of hypertension and rheumatism were also higher.

Local epics also describe giving birth with the help of the stones. The Nart saga of the Adyghe describes Sataney-Guasha who gave birth to the central hero of the epic in an unusual way. One of the Nart shepherds, who was captivated by Sataney-Guasha's beauty and was unable to get to her through the river that separated them, shot an arrow (carrying his sperm) across the shore to Sataney-Guasha. Sinking into the coastal rock, the arrow impregnated it. Then an image of a human boy appeared on the stone, and a local blacksmith carved this image of the boy from the stone on behalf of Sataney-Guasha. He attached it to her body, and after a while he turned into a man and was named Sasrykva.

Russian scientist A. Dubrov studied the influence of EMF on human organisms and showed that EMF affects the physiology of the female body, such as the course of the menstrual cycle, labor activity, and toxicosis of pregnancy.[33] Some authors also believe that geomagnetic field (GMF) activity also affects the onset of menstruation in women and the course of labor. It turns out that the rhythm of both the beginning and the end of labor depends on the daily rhythm of the GMF. A number of cases noted that the frequency of the GMF oscillations coincided with brain rhythms and the frequency of smooth muscle vibrations. At the same time, there is a direct correlation between the frequency of births and the strength of the GMF, which is most noticeable on the 2nd, 9th, and 13th days after a disturbance in the earth's magnetic field.[34]

Fedorov showed that the influence of this unknown factor has been significant, even in recent times. For example, a higher population in Inner Dagestan, in the Chechen Republic, in the 18th century was noted after part of the population migrated to Transcaucasia; military activity also increased. In the 19th century, Dagestan was one of the most overcrowded regions of Russia. A similar sharp increase in population in the 18th century was noted in Chechnya during the beginning of organized military forays. At present, Ingushetia leads Russia in terms of population growth. All these republics are located in the region of the highest tectonic activities.

Apparently, population growth is related to the effect of an unknown geological factor on biological objects, that is, on humans. Perhaps such an impact caused an extraordinary increase in the population in the Altai region of Mongolia, from which crowds of conquerors came.[35] What if dolmens were built to boost human reproductivity in the North Caucasus area? What if the ancients knew some completely forgotten natural laws that contributed to this effect?

Other applications of the dolmen's infrasound-generating ability that several other authors suggested range from being some sort of a mental weapon, long-distance information transmitting device, seismograph, healing equipment, or earthquake prevention device.

I think, that the dolmens' ability to act as energy amplifiers was used by shamans (let's call them "operators"). Instead of tuning up every dolmen according to some specific pattern, an operator may simply be in the inner chamber when the dolmen starts vibrating due to natural triggers, such as the tidal actions of the moon and sun. Operators could simply embed their thoughts (or even some kind of spell casting) into the dolmen's energy, thereby broadcasting their thoughts to the local population over a long distance with great power.

Imagine these thousands of dolmens tuned up to one specific thought and working together in unison. What mighty effect could this have produced? There could have been other applications of such energy other than boosting progress and increasing births.

The human mind is a receptacle as well as a transmitter, and receives as well as broadcasts. We may refer to this technology today as mind control, social engineering, or social control. Social engineering, within the context of mind control, is a way to gradually and subtly manipulate, coerce, or influence a segment of the population. This is most effectively achieved at the subconscious level.[36] Mind control has been known since ancient times and control techniques include rituals, cults, and simple propaganda; modern armies work on so-called "psychological warfare." Propaganda, threats, and other psychological techniques are used to mislead, intimidate, demoralize, or otherwise influence someone's thinking or behavior.

In 1973, Dr. Joseph Sharp of the Walter Reed Army Institute of Research successfully demonstrated "voice to skull transmission." This used artificial microwaves and a computer to control a radar transmitter sending out a single pulse that was heard inside a test subject's head as a "click." These pulses, or clicks, were actually trained to the timing of the human voice waveform, which then resulted in a voice being heard inside the head, rather than a series of clicks.

Continued research into the use of microwaves and behavior modification caught academic attention in 1975 when Dr. Don R. Justesen published an article titled "Microwaves and Behavior" in the March issue of *American Psychologist*. Justesen is credited with "laying a larger foundation for the use of pulsed microwave radiation as a method of controlling people." Justesen wrote that the sounds heard "were not unlike those emitted by persons with artificial larynxes,"[37] and that they were simple words, not complex, as more complex words would require more energy to transmit and possibly approach or surpass the limit of safe exposure.

Law enforcement uses a Long Range Acoustic Device (LRAD) that emits sound waves to quiet crowds and keep riots under control as well as to cease violent behavior by temporarily disorienting the intended victims. O. Volkov, in a 1999 article in the Russian journal *The Voice of the Universe*, indicated that Russia is testing psychological warfare on citizens, because "Western society, Western people are legally protected from directed psycho-influence, but ours are not." He also complained that in Russia the tasks of managing its people and reducing their numbers are being simultaneously solved with this warfare, as well as testing such expensive psi-technologies on its own citizens. As we can see, the tradition of using psychotropic technologies on common people indeed continues today.

Whatever the reason ancient builders had for erecting the dolmens, they obviously invested a lot of energy and ingenuity in their construction. Therefore, dolmens must have been very important to our ancestors.

Ancient Dark Retreat or "Prisoner Movie Cinema"

Based on many ancient records, spiritual traditions around the world used darkness in the pursuit of enlightenment. Underground caves, catacombs, and pyramids are some examples of places that provided total darkness. Probably since the beginning of time, spiritual seekers sought places to spend time in total darkness and achieve mystical connection.

To attain this intimate unity with God or Nature, one has to go on a solo retreat in a place that is completely absent of light. The Kogi people of Colombia, in order to achieve enlightenment, spent 18 years in dark caves or huts. Select boys lived in a dark cave for the first nine years of their lives as part of special training to become enlightened ones. Elder Kogi priests and the child's mother cared for, fed, and trained them. Before the boys entered the outside world, they were attuned to Aluna, or the "Great Mother," who was their creator figure. The boys were being trained as priests in order to support the balance of harmony and creativity in the world.[38] Total darkness is also practiced in Taoism, the Dzogchen tradition of the Nyingma school of Tibetan Buddhism, ancient Tibetan Bönpo shamanism, and other schools of Tibetan Buddhism.

Russian science fiction author Ivan Efremov described in 1963 the feelings of someone who went through the total darkness ritual in Tibet:

It was necessary to tear off the person who was completely connected with the surrounding world from all the sensations that filled his mind. Even the feeling of passing time disappeared—seconds, hours, minutes, days, and nights were no different from all the previous, dissolved in formless gloom. Time stopped! And the person imprisoned here seemed that he was standing at the very brink of being, looking behind this veil of bizarre patterns that are woven by Maya ("illusion" in Indian philosophy), a mirage of life from all senses, man in his oneness with nature. According to the idea of ancient ascetics, the prisoner must be cleansed of everything that prevented him from departing from his vain life, so that the soul, polished as a mirror, could reflect the whole depth of space.[39]

In order to achieve this special state of mind in the pursuit of enlightenment, many spiritual traditions have used darkness—a very powerful tool for such purposes. Darkness stimulates our imagination, forcing the human soul to "remember" primordial fears, as well as frees the soul from its connection to the material world, thus creating psychic realms. Qigong master Mantak Chia provides a scientific explanation of how our consciousness reacts, based on the number of days spent in total darkness:

The darkness actualizes successively higher states of divine consciousness, correlating with the synthesis and accumulation of psychedelic chemicals in the brain. Melatonin, a regulatory hormone, quiets the body and mind in preparation for the finer and subtler realities of higher consciousness (days 1 to 3).

Pinoline, affecting the neuro-transmitters of the brain, permits visions and dream-states to emerge in our conscious awareness (days 3 to 5). Eventually, the brain synthesizes the "spirit molecules" 5-methoxy-dimethyltryptamine (5-MeO-DMT) and dimethyltryptamine (DMT), facilitating the transcendental experiences of universal love and compassion (days 6 to 12).

Melatonin, the "sleep molecule," is produced in the pineal gland in response to the darkness of night and to the circadian rhythms of light and dark that are programmed into the hypothalamus, an endocrine gland located deep within the brain. Melatonin affects major organ systems, quieting the sympathetic nervous system and allowing daily rejuvenation of mind and body.[40]

The period of time necessary for a dark retreat ranges from a few hours to several decades. Because there is total absence of optical stimulation, one can experience "prisoner's cinema," commonly known as the *lights*. The prisoner's cinema is a phenomenon experienced by prisoners kept in dark cells for long time. The "movie" is similar to the "light show" of various colors that a prisoner can "see." It is difficult to describe. Scientists explain that this is a result of phosphenes (we will talk about phosphenes later in the book), which are the psychological effects of a long time without light. Astronauts who are exposed to certain types of radiation can experience similar effects.

Modern-day retreats in total darkness are called Kaya Kalpa retreats in India. The term *kaya* means "body" and *kalpa* means "ageless," or "immortal." *Kaya Kalpa* literally means "ageless body" (or "body fashioning").

According to "dark room retreat" adepts, spending some time in total darkness will rejuvenate your body, slow the aging process, and allow you to see into the past and future. You will understand the true meaning of existence and the order of things. This is like returning to the womb or to nature's original darkness.

Some scientists suggest that a connection exists between the prisoner's cinema phenomenon and Neolithic cave paintings. Viewing phosphenes after spending some time in a dark dolmen could have played a role in shamanic ritual practices.

North Caucasus dolmens are perfect structures for practicing total-darkness techniques. Constructed with such precision that a knife blade can't be inserted between the blocks, and with an entrance hole closed by a plug, the dolmen can provide total darkness. Anyone who is inside cannot interrupt their "imprisonment" by simply pushing out the plug. Besides being heavy, the plug was fixed in the hole by mud or other means.

I think that people who practiced such techniques for either healing purposes or "reading" the future constructed the dolmens. An ancient belief says that there is a "database," called the *Akashic* records, of all human events, thoughts, words, and emotions—past, present, and future. We may no longer know how to connect to these records, but ancient peoples may have known, practiced this technique, and "downloaded" necessary information. For this purpose, megalithic peoples built dolmens in order to surround themselves with total darkness. What if dolmens were really just ancient "dark room retreats"?

How the Blocks Were Quarried and Processed

As seen in the previous chapters, dolmens look similar to other megaliths around the world. Based on this observation, we may assume that they might have been built by the same people or by people with the same knowledge of quarrying, processing, transporting, and mounting huge megalithic blocks. This chapter explores the technologies that ancient megalith builders may have known and used.

Location of Dolmen Quarries

Dolmen researchers U. Sharikov and O. Komissar described in their work how they tried to find quarries where dolmen blocks could have been made.[1] Quarries where megalith stones might have come from usually have the remains of either unfinished pieces of stone or traces of mining (that is, grooves or furrows in the stone, Figure 54).

They explored several places that local historians identified as "ancient quarries" near the village of Pshada in the Gelendzhik district, Kamenny Karier (Stone Quarry) quarry in the Tuapse region, the village of Erivanskaya in the Abinsky District, and others, and did not find signs of quarries there. In fact, these turned out to be natural sandstone outcrops. However, they found that these sandstone outcrops were not very common. What was unusual about them?

Figure 54. Stone marks at one of the megalith quarries in Axum, Ethiopia.

Sharikov and Komissar explained that sandstone is a sedimentary rock formed after precipitation destroys rocks in bodies of water. The characteristic feature of sedimentary rocks is their stratification (stratum). The stratum is a layer of sedimentary rock whose composition is more or less the same throughout and that is visibly different from the rock layers above and below it (Figure 55, left).

Figure 55. Typical stratum of sedimentary rock, left. Rocky outcrop of sandstone near Bytkha at Jackal Rocks, right.

Outcrops of sandstone that local ethnographers pointed to as the "ancient quarries" in question did not have a layered structure characteristic of sedimentary rocks, but represented bizarre arrays, with signs of flows and covers, as if the "sand lava" had erupted and froze. None of the places mentioned as ancient quarries contained traces of stone marks. Therefore, they were not ancient quarries. However, near each dolmen or cluster of dolmens were places where sandstone existed as if it were frozen lava (Figure 54, right).

The average weight of the typical dolmen is 15 to 30 metric tons, although there are dolmens in which the covering block itself weighs about 20 metric tons. The amount of mined sandstone for the construction of this single dolmen, taking into account the production and transport waste, would be approximately 40 to 60 metric tons. Consequently, the territory of the Western Caucasus should have quarries as old as the dolmens with, roughly counting, a total capacity of 1,200,000 to 1,800,000 metric tons.[2] How could an entire industry in the early Bronze Age not leave a trace of such production?

Some researchers suggest that the blocks the builders needed to construct the dolmens were found ready and only had to be transported to the construction site and processed in place. In fact, the marl beds (beds formed from the disintegration of the rock and the accumulation of the remains of shells, animals, and plants, resulting in a mixture of sand, magnesium, iron, clay, azote, and limestone) contain sandstone layers of suitable thickness, but the stratum of suitable sizes, approximately 2 x 3 m (6.5 x 9.8 ft.), is extremely rare. Then the problem of transporting stone slabs over mountains as high as 870 m (2,854 ft.) above sea level as well as through gorges with no roads for long distances is no less complex than the splitting of stone.

To this day, the quarrying method for these blocks and the processing to the desired size remain unclear.

Wooden Wedges

Often in archaeology books and works, the technique ancient builders used to split stones is described as the "wooden wedges" method, in which dry wedges were inserted into grooves, wetted, and then allowed to swell overnight, splitting the stone. In the book *The Art of Splitting Stone*, the authors discuss several significant details about this method and make the case for using both iron and wooden wedges together.[3]

Several stones left by ancient dolmen builders have groove patterns. Similar grooves patterns can be observed in ancient quarries around the world, such as in Egypt, and grooves have been found on a few blocks left near dolmens (Figure 56).

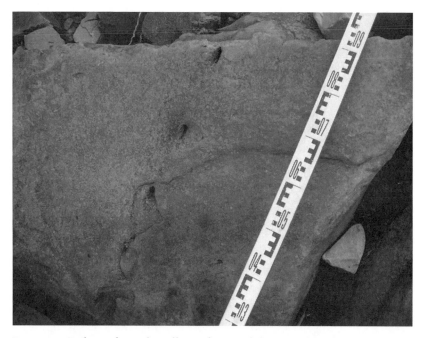

Figure 56. Dolmen from the village of Vozrozhdenie, Gelendzhik area, showing chiseled hole marks.

Therefore, to use this method, ancient builders had to make the grooves long enough to be able to split wide and thick stone blocks. Next, water had to be put on the wooden wedges to make them swell until the rock split. This method may work well for relatively thin rocks, but what about large, thick rocks? German researchers described one such attempt to split a large rock:

> The thesis was advanced that stone blocks with damp wooden wedges were blasted from the stone. This thesis, frequently presented in writings must be strongly challenged and was inspected by members of the association Hobby-Ägyptologen e.V. The limestone used for this test weighed 450 kg and came from a quarry near the city of Aachen. The scratch test with drops of diluted hydrochloric acid, which reacts to stone blocks with the intense formation of fizzing blisters, confirmed for us that this was a block of limestone (calcite).

Experiment:

Using a drill and steel chisel, four wedge holes were made in an experiment block over 12 hours. The wooden wedges corresponding to the wedge hole were driven into the wedge holes with a sledge hammer and dampened with a water sprinkling system for 100 hours. Three removal attempts with different types of wooden wedges (cedar, oak and beechwood) were conducted. Only dry wooden wedges were used, which were optimized by drying in the oven at 100° C to remove the remaining moisture.

Result:

...the blocks did not split. Through this experiment, we additionally learned that the pyramid builders were never able to create exact wedge holes with their stone axes due to the enormous amount of time it would have taken. An attempt was started with a refurbished bronze chisel which was interrupted after 30 minutes as the chisel was blunted without leaving a trace on the block. As the previous experiment described shows, the idea that the pyramid builders know the wedge technology for removing the blocks must be refuted. In our subsequent research, we did not find a single trace of half wedge holes, which should be visible on the unprocessed blocks. The traces of wedge holes on the loose blocks which lay around the Giza pyramids were left by stone robbers in the Middle Ages and/or are recent, from when the pyramids were used as a quarry for the creation of Cairo. (Galerie Laemmer)[4] (Figure 57)

That means that either all the necessary blocks of the exact thickness were present for the wedges method, or ancient builders used some other unknown method to split large rocks. I think that the chiseled hole marks (Figure 56) were left in modern times by people who were trying to use dolmen blocks for local construction projects.

More than 2,000 dolmens made of blocks have been found in the Caucasus. The question is why it is extremely rare to find any fragments

Figure 57. Stone block with wooden wedges inserted.

of the megalith makers' construction activity. If found, fragments of the blocks would clearly testify to their separation from the original rock. Further, the edges of many dolmen blocks are rounded (Figure 58). Random stones with traces of splitting attempts by wedges are rare and often belong to completely different historical epochs. Perhaps the

Figure 58. Rounded edges of blocks of the central dolmen in the Okhara and Kapibga dolmen complex.

ancient builders used a completely different method to produce the rectangular dolmen blocks.

Also, due to the absence of stones of the desired thickness, we will later discuss how the dolmen builders may not even have required mining and splitting huge stone blocks.

Stone Softening

Some parts of dolmens have strange patterns that don't look like tool-marks but which are similar to prints on a soft surface (Figures 59, 60, and 61). If ancient builders knew how to soften stones, that may provide answers to the many unanswered questions regarding how the dolmens were built.

Figure 59. Dolmen "Strong Woman," left. Fragment of the portal of the dolmen, right. Achibs River (Pshada village)

Various dolmens have many similar and interesting patterns (Figures 62, 63, 64, 65, 66). It may not be possible to make such intricate shapes and bas-reliefs using a flake technique (discussed later in the "Percussion and Pressure Flaking Technique" section).

Shaping such blocks using only round stone hammers seems unlikely. There are, however, a few theories about how the blocks were shaped. Local legends in South America talk about a liquid known to the ancients, derived from plants, that can soften rocks. Explorers such as Percy Fawcett also brought back tales of such a substance. In his book *Exploration Fawcett: Journey to the Lost City of Z*, he talks of birds that

Figure 60. One of the dolmens from the "city of dolmens" near the village of Erivanskaya on the left bank of the river Abin. Inset, closeup of the surface.

Figure 61. Another example of a pattern on a dolmen near Lazarevsky City District. Inset, closeup of the fragment.

Figure 62. Dolmen from Leso-Kyafar (Karachay-Cherkessia) in the Stavropol Museum with an intricate bas-relief. Possible toolmarks on soft material appear on the left side.

Figure 63. Dolmen at Psynako 1 megalithic complex.

Figure 64. Dolmen near Prigorodny village of the Tuapse region, left; closeup of a false plug in a dolmen in the "Wolf Gate" group, right.

Figure 65. Dolmen blocks that appear as if they were soft at the time of connection. Dolmen on Mount Nexis, left; dolmen from the Kizinka tract, center; dolmen from the village of Noviy (New), right.

Figure 66. Dolmen with a false plug in the Pitsunda area. The dolmen was moved to a local museum from the village of Esher.

would use leaves to soften stones in order to peck a hole for a nest there. He explains that a bird makes a hole in the rock like a woodpecker makes a hole in a tree. Before starting to peck, the bird rubs the leaves in a circular motion over the rock surface. It does this three or four times with fresh leaves. Then it starts pecking at the rock and goes through the rubbing process with leaves several times before continuing to peck. It takes several days, but finally the bird opens a hole deep enough for a nest. Fawcett also talks about a plant a foot (30 cm) high with dark reddish leaves that the Incas used to shape stones.[5]

Hiram Bingham III, who discovered Machu Picchu, also talked about such a plant, and in 1983, Catholic priest Jorge A. Lira asserted that he had reproduced this stone softening ability (although he was unable to figure out how to make the stones hard again).[6]

Spanish chronicler Diego de Rosales, in his 1674 work *Historia General del Reino de Chile*, describes Mapuche Indian medicinal plants and speaks of an herb called *pito*, one of the rarest in the world and which has great medicinal value.

A more modern article, presented at the 21st International Symposium on Archaeometry (ISA) in 1981, states:

The starting stone material (silicate or silico-aluminate) is dissolved by the organic extracts, and the viscous slurry is then poured into a mold where it hardens. This technique, when mastered, allows a sort of cement to be made by dissolving rocks; statues which could have been made by the technique of the pre-Incan Huanaka, by dissolution followed by geopolymeric agglomeration, are found to contain Caoxalate in the stone.[7]

They even presented at the meeting some actual samples of stone that had dissolved and been reaggregated:

The great surprise was actually to discover very ancient references to their use since Neolithic times for working materials which are very hard but easily attacked by acids, such as chalk. Thus, a bas-relief from the tomb of Mera, at Saqqarah (VI dynasty, 3 Millennium BC, Egypt) shows the hollowing out of "Egyptian alabaster" (CaC03) vases by a liquid contained in a water skin or bladder. An experiment of interest was to compare the "bio-tooling" technique with the shaping of a hole using a steel tool and the quartz sand technique recommended by pre-historians. The hole resulting from sand abrasion has rough walls, whereas bio-tooling gives a smooth finish.[8]

The ancient dolmen builders were probably capable of producing the necessary quantities of the same acids Davidovits used in his experiments from plants that were common to the region in the past. They may have used the following technique to work the stones: the stones were quarried, then broken or crushed into manageable sizes for transportation to the mountains, and then reaggregated in situ while being cast into the megalithic slabs we now see.

Soft Sedimentary Rock Method

In my travels I have seen many places around the world that have "cart ruts," which are parallel tracks running through hard rock (Figure 65). While discussing the mystery of these tracks is beyond the scope of this book, it is important to know that the stone in which these ruts exist was probably soft at one time.

One method ancient builders might have used to acquire dolmen blocks was to literally make them in situ from soft rock that became hard with time or after special treatment. In a 2017 article in the *Crimean Telegraph*, archaeologist Lovpache Nurbiy indicated:

Recently, U. Sharikov and O. Komissar published a book about how dolmens were molded. It was based on geological data that, at that time, a clay-sand plastic mass of approximately 200 degrees Celsius [392 degrees Fahrenheit] was squeezed out onto the surface from a great depth in the ground. After about two weeks in this mud condition, it froze. This, however, applies only to sandstone dolmens.[8]

Figure 67. Author investigating cart ruts in Malta.

The "plastic" version can also explain the creation of monolithic dolmens, especially the making of the monolithic dolmen chambers. These chambers could only have been made through an "entrance" hole with a diameter of 30 to 40 cm (11.8 to 15.7 in.). This can also explain the construction of dolmens from megaton slabs as well as the lack of tools and characteristic quarries. But could the stone rocks have been in a "plastic" state in a relatively recent historical period, when the construction of dolmens is considered to have been between the fourth and second millennia BC?

Geologist V. N. Kholodov studied the processes of formation and surface exit of a nonlayered structure of sandstone in the Azov-Kuban Basin. He came to the conclusion that under favorable conditions, at a depth of five to six km (3.1 to 3.7 miles) in clay strata, under the influence of high temperature and pressure, complex solutions are formed, which are squeezed into faults and which rush to the earth's surface like mud volcanoes. This is the clay-sand mass, which freezes over several days on the surface (Figure 68). Such eruptions can now be found in the west of Turkmenistan. The local population calls them "Shaytan gardens" (Devil gardens). Judging by the remnants of formless blocks of sandstone in many places in the Caucasus, this happened only a few thousand years ago.[9]

Figure 68. A wall inside of a semimonolithic dolmen where the wall material has cracked, probably at the time of drying (dolmen on the Nechepsuho River, near the White Rocks waterfall, village Novomikhailovskaya, in the Tuapse region).

Authors U. Sharikov and O. Komissar, on the basis of Kholodov's work and their own experiment on dolmen molding, conclude that the ancient inhabitants of these places built dolmens in this particular way.[10] If this is so, then the transportation of giant multitonnage plates and their careful adjustment to each other could be easily explained.

The end of these geological processes led to the decline of the dolmen culture, and later megaliths are more primitive.

Concrete Casting Technique

Marks on some of the dolmens curiously resemble modern concrete, indicating that they were molded to give them a shape. Perhaps ancient builders did not transport giant stone blocks for miles from quarries to the construction site but used the casting method. That is, individual elements of the dolmen were cast from the sand-cement mass. They made a desired form in the ground and modeled the blocks of the dolmen.

The side blocks of many dolmens (about 92 percent of all dolmens) have a characteristic lenticular shape on the cut that bulges outward. The inner surface of the block is flat. The ends of the blocks, which should have been cut down, processed, and customized, look like completely natural stone. The upper surfaces of such blocks are rounded and do not have traces of processing. The block edges also sharply end, as if the solution was poured or laid in a casting (Figure 69). However, this theory may not be plausible for all types of dolmens because their

Figure 69. A dolmen on a farm on the Doguab River, left. On the lower edge of the cover plate (rear), a clear boundary is visible, formed by the principle of spreading a plastic mass along a solid horizontal surface. The end of the plate has a rounded shape and does not carry traces of stone cutting or stone processing. Right, a dolmen on Mount Tsigankova (Pshada) whose side plates have a characteristic lenticular shape and convex outward.

blocks were made from different materials, such as granite, sandstone, or limestone.

Of course, the dolmen builders could use the "glacial erratics" left in the area during the Ice Age. A glacial erratic is a piece of rock that differs from the size and type of rock native to the area in which it is found and which was carried by glacial ice over hundreds of miles. Erratics can easily be large boulders; one side of this boulder is flat, the effect of dragging for long distances over hard surfaces. The question is where the builders found so many erratics of the necessary size.

Plaster Casting Technique

Plastering, sometimes called *stucco*, refers to construction or ornamentation done with plaster, such as a layer of plaster on an interior or exterior wall structure, or plaster decorative moldings on ceilings or walls. Stucco is applied wet and hardens to a very dense solid. It may be used to cover less visually appealing construction materials such as concrete, stone, clay brick, and adobe. It is possible that dolmen builders knew about this technique and used it to create dolmen bas-reliefs and decorations.

Some of the dolmens display the marks of possible stucco, as if the structure was plastered after construction, and then over time the coating fell off in places (Figure 70).

Figure 70. Dolmen from Vozrozhdenie village, left; dolmen on the Janet River, right.

The marks on the dolmens do not look like the natural process of stone detachment because the detachment is not uniform. The contour of the bas-relief should also be visible under the fallen "plaster." However, this is not the case. The surface under the detachment is flat and looks like the bas-relief was molded on damp plaster.

Using this technique does not require painstakingly removing unwanted parts of the stone block in order to leave only the necessary decoration. Because stucco is applied wet and hardens to a dense solid, this technique could have been used for creating false plugs.

Processing the Blocks

The inner and outer surfaces of the front of the dolmens are very smooth. Some dolmens have simple geometric ornaments and bas-reliefs that stand out against the background of the surface. Each block from which the dolmens are built connects to another one with great precision. How were ancient builders able to achieve such accuracy and quality?

It is generally accepted that stone blocks are cut from the stone massif. Then they are given the necessary form, which has certain proportions and sizes determined by the size of the dolmen as a whole and the dimensions of the adjacent plates in particular (side, cover, front, and back blocks). The question is why the external surfaces of the stone blocks and their ends do not display any traces of stone splitting and processing?

Moreover, during archaeological excavations, scientists were unable to find any tools that can be identified as being used for processing the blocks. As before, we will explore orthodox and unorthodox methods that dolmen builders could have used to achieve these results.

Percussion and Pressure Flaking Technique

According to mainstream archaeology, ancient people were familiar and skillful with stone tools to make other stone tools for treating stone surfaces. Stone tools were produced in two main ways: percussion and pressure. Percussion flaking (chipping off pieces of stone) can be done either by striking a piece of stone with a harder stone, wood, or bone held in the hand, or by hitting the piece itself on the edge of the fixed stone. The latter method is called the anvil method. Using a wooden workpiece or bar allows you to remove longer, thinner, and flatter parts of the stone. Because the wood is resilient, it does not destroy the edge of the stone, and it leaves smaller and flatter holes. The detachment under pressure, as the name implies, is to push with a pointed stick or bone near the edge of the stone to separate the small pieces from both sides. This method was used mainly to provide a final look to the tools or to create the desired shape.

Soviet scientist Sergey Semenov, an authority in ancient stone manufacturing techniques, described, among other technologies, how ancient people used percussion flaking to make various stone tools and constructions.[11] Apparently, this was a common technique for treating stone surfaces to make them smooth.

However, Semenov also pointed out that not all rocks were treated with the flaking technique. Flint, quartzite, obsidian, quartz, chalcedony, and other stones with a rugged fracture, are fragile, sensitive to impact, and succumb poorly to this method. The main materials that survive the percussion flaking technique are rocks that contain volcanic sulfur: basalt, diorite, granodiorite, syenite, gabbro, labradorite, diabase, porphyry, and sandstone.[12]

The main feature of the percussion technique was using light tapping blows to remove small particles of rock from the surface of a raw stone block. The dolmen block material belongs to granular rocks that include particles of quartz, feldspar, biotite, muscovite, and mica and should naturally be treated more easily than shales or diorites that have a more homogeneous structure (Figure 71). One wonders how long it might take to prepare the surface of one block for constructing a dolmen?

Experiments Semenov performed established that 30 to 45 g (0.07 to 0.1 lb.) of granite, 30 to 35 g (0.0.7 to 0.08 lb.) of basalt, and 25 to 30 g (0.06 to 0.07 lb.) of nephrite were removed in an hour of operation

Figure 71. Inner surface of one of the dolmens that looks like it may have been treated with percussion flaking (dolmen in the village of Vozrozhdenie on the Janet River).

using a pounder weighing 250 to 300 g (0.55-0.66 lb.). Up to 120 blows per minute were often applied with a very short trajectory (5-10 cm or 2-4 in.). In total, 7,200 strokes were applied in an hour and only 4 to 5 mg of rock fell from each blow. Increasing the weight of the pounder to 1.5 to 2 kg (3.3 to 4.4 lb.), the number of beats per minute did not really decrease, and the weight unit of the falling particles increased. Using a diabase striker of 5 kg (11 lb.) with impacts from a height of 10 to 15 cm (4-8 in.) with 60 beats per minute, 400-500 g (0.9-1.1 lb.) of hard limestone were removed in one hour of operation.[13]

Using the percussion technique was apparently the main method for processing stone faces when iron was not yet used. In places where granite obelisks were dressed (such as in Egypt), balls of dolerite (a kind of a basalt) covered with scrapes from numerous impacts were found. Their weight averaged 5 to 6 kg (11 to 13 lb.) and the diameter was from 12 to 30 cm (4.7 to 11 in.), so it was possible to work with such a "hammer" only with both hands.[14] There is no doubt that the dolerite balls

Figure 72. Ball found in a dolmen near the village of Shepsi.

were used to dress the obelisk faces until they were as flat as possible. Murals depicting scenes of working on the decoration of stone blocks and large statues show the worker with a ball in both hands. Were not some of these stone balls found in one of the dolmens (Figure 72)?

However, not all the peculiarities of dressing dolmen blocks and construction techniques can be explained with such simple and logical methods. Other simple methods of dressing stones and constructing and transporting megalithic blocks may not have survived to the present day.

Shamir

The first Jewish temple in Jerusalem was built using huge monoliths, many of which were much larger than the blocks used in constructing dolmens. As described in the Old Testament, because Moses had commanded the Israelites not to use "any tool of iron" in the construction of holy places, Solomon ordered that no hammers, axes, or chisels should be used to cut and dress the massive stone blocks for building the outer walls and courtyard of the temple. Instead, he provided the artisans with an ancient device dating back to the time of Moses himself.[15]

The device was called a *shamir* and was capable of cutting the toughest of materials without friction or heat. Also known as "the stone that splits rocks," the shamir was not to be placed in an iron or metal vessel for safekeeping, as "it would burst such a receptacle asunder. It is kept wrapped up in a woolen cloth, and this in turn is placed in a lead basket filled with barley bran";[16] the shamir possessed "the remarkable property of cutting the hardest of diamonds."

According to Immanuel Velikovsky,[17] the shamir "reportedly could disintegrate anything, even hard, durable stones." King Solomon was eager to possess the shamir because he had heard about it from earlier days; knowledge of the shamir is in fact ascribed by rabbinical sources to Moses. After much searching, a grain of shamir the size of a barleycorn was found in a distant country, in the depths of a well, and brought to Solomon. But strangely, it lost its abilities and became inactive several centuries later, about the time the Temple of Solomon was destroyed by Nebuchadnezzar. With the destruction of the temple, the shamir has vanished.

The "orthodox" time that modern archaeologists accept for when the dolmens were erected (between the fourth and the second millennia BC) is not far from the time Solomon's temple was built in Jerusalem, when the shamir was pretty much "in power." Was it possible that ancient dolmen builders used a shamir for cutting and dressing the dolmen stones?

Making the Dolmen Entrance

Archaeological finds demonstrating the phases in manufacturing the entrance are extremely rare. However, such exemplars still exist (Figures 73 and 74).

An unfinished entrance hole was found on the facade block of a monolith dolmen near the village of Erivanskaya. Made at a depth of about 10 cm (3.9 in.), it had smooth walls along the perimeter of the

Figure 73. Unfinished tiled dolmen in the "Wolf Gate" tract (red arrow is pointing to the unfinished entrance).

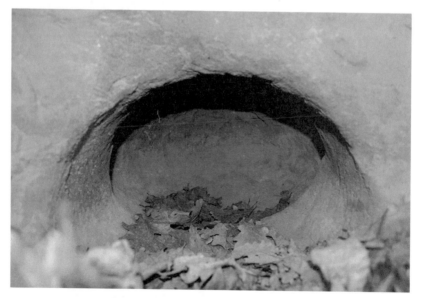

Figure 74. Unfinished entrance to a dolmen at the village of Erivanskaya.

circle, and the bottom of the formed cylinder was chaotically chopped. Apparently, the hole was not drilled, but cut out along the perimeter, while the inner part of the stone was broken into pieces, providing the opportunity to go further into the rock.

How laborious was processing blocks for dolmens to create an entrance hole or bas-relief? For this purpose, researchers conducted experiments to discover the possible technology for the surface treatment by using sandstone similar in quality to dolmen blocks.

For the experiment of processing the portal plate, the researchers decided to use a flint tool as a cutter. Also, for proof of the technologies, tools of diabase, copper, and bronze were involved. When making the rounded perimeter of the future entrance, flint was found to be the most effective tool.[18]

The abrasive properties of the sandstone led the metal tool to quickly get blunt and lose its effectiveness. Flint and diabase lasted much longer. It should be noted that diabase is more acceptable for percussive work, as it is a less fragile stone, whereas the flint is clearly superior for carving. In two hours of working with a flint cutter, a stone chopper, and a copper adze, the researchers were able to cut to a depth of 30 mm (1.1 in.). As A. Kizilov noted, this technique of working with stone proved to be effective for creating convex bas-relief patterns on the frontal plate.[19]

The Incredible Sciences of the Ancients

There are strong biases that ancient peoples had unsophisticated technology and rudimentary material cultures. However, many archaeological findings debunk such prejudices. Siberian archaeologists found a 40,000-year-old bracelet in a cave in Denisova in the Altai Territory. The bracelet was made of polished stone of a mica-like mineral of chlorite (Figure 75, left). To create an artificial hole in this Siberian chlorite bracelet required a high-speed drill of some kind, which was impossible at that time, according to modern preconceptions.

Modern-day archaeologists have found many of those anomalous artifacts. Just a couple of examples are the Greek Antikythera device

Figure 75. Bracelet made of polished stone, left; Greek Antikythera device, right.

(Figure 75, right), a second-century BC analog computer, or even Baghdad's third-century AD electric battery.

Whatever technologies the ancient builders had, we can clearly see that they were capable of creating complex shapes and bas-reliefs. Dolmens invite us to learn more about our past and to realize that the ancients might have been far more advanced than we give them credit for.

Transporting the Megalithic Blocks

A s previously discussed, the question of where ancient builders could take huge stone blocks remains unanswered. After producing blocks, they needed to be transported to where the dolmens would be built. Since dolmens stand in mountain terrain, before ancient peoples could start building the dolmens, they had to solve the complex transport problem. How did they deliver multiton stone blocks to the construction site in a mountainous area with no roads?

I have already suggested several methods for building dolmens that did not require transporting huge blocks, however, this section will review other possible methods ancient builders could have used to transfer the megalithic blocks and put them in place.

The Push-Pull Method

The push-pull method has been used since ancient times. Egyptian pyramid builders used this method to transport huge statues, obelisks, and construction blocks (Figure 76).

Because North Caucasus dolmens have similar construction characteristics to ancient Egypt (see Table 1), we may presume that dolmen builders may have used a similar method.

Moving large stones overland was a very difficult task. We assume that sledges and rollers were probably already known in those distant

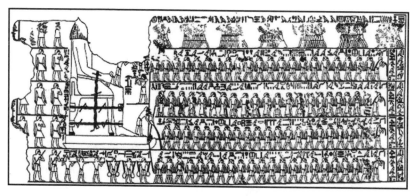

Figure 76. Moving a statue in Twelfth Dynasty Egypt.

times and that the necessary workers were available in large numbers. However, the main obstacle was friction. You can roughly calculate how much force is needed to move a block weighing 10 metric tons—the average weight of the dolmen plate—if you pull this slab on wooden rollers up a hill with a slope of 15 degrees.

The coefficient of friction when sliding a stone on a tree is equal to 0.46-0.60.[1] The builders of dolmens could use lubricant to reduce the friction and reduce the slip coefficient. For our calculations, we use a coefficient of friction equal to 0.5. Then, moving the stone block in a horizontal position would require an effort of 5 metric tons (10,000 * 0.5).

If you pull the plate uphill along an inclined plane at an angle of 15 degrees, a force of 2,590 kg (10 metric tons multiplied by a sine of 15 degrees—10,000 * 0.258) is added. In total, to drag such a block uphill takes an effort of about 7.5 metric tons (5,000 + 2,590 = 7,590 kg). If one person can drag up to 40 kg (88 lb.), therefore it will take 188 people to drag the block (7,500 / 40).

But the friction of rest is greater than the friction of motion, so almost twice as many people will need to start moving this block! If the plate weighs more than 10 metric tons, more people will be needed, respectively.

Thus, a 10-ton block of a dolmen block could require 350 to 400 people. Maybe the builders of dolmens used draft animals, and then the number of people required could have been smaller.

As some of the leading dolmen researchers estimate, to construct one average-size dolmen requires producing approximately 40 to 60 metric tons of sandstone (taking into consideration sandstone waste during production and transportation). Therefore, considering the estimated number of dolmens (30,000) that existed in the North Caucasus, mining about 1,200,000 to 1,800,000 metric tons from ancient sandstone quarries would be required. This is, of course, a rough calculation. The North Caucasus doesn't have large quantities of sandstone resources, or transportation. One natural source of sandstone is located 40 to 50 km (28 to 32 miles) from some dolmens. To transport 60 metric tons for 30 miles through rough terrain sometimes to a height of up to 900 m (3,000 ft.) is not trivial, even by today's standards. How did dolmen builders achieve this?

Russian researcher Vladimir Marcovin suggests that this was done using an old "classic" method: "Now the blocks are cut down. They must be delivered to the place. And with the help of rollers (of equal form logs), ropes, human and bull strength, they dragged the material to the chosen corner, where the dolmen would be erected. The method is very ancient."[2]

Based on this estimate, to transport 60 metric tons of stone, dolmen builders required 120 men or 12 oxen for one dolmen. Here we are talking about 120 to 150 strong men altogether, specialists in road construction, mining stone from quarries, cutting wood for sledges, and builder-masons (Markovin didn't take into consideration the friction discussed above). This was possible only in a highly organized society with a well-established economic infrastructure.

According to the calculations of Soviet archaeologist V. Pachulia, one dolmen had to be built every one to two years.[3] If several dolmens had to be built simultaneously, it would require multiple men or oxen. However, according to mainstream archaeologists, the age of dolmen building was at the beginning of the Bronze Age, where only tribal relations existed and a tribe consisted of between 40 and 60 people.

On the Indonesian Island of Sumba, the practice of building megalithic tombs similar to the Caucasus dolmens has survived until mod-

Figure 77. Moving a block of stone as part of a ritual on Nias Island in Indonesia.

ern times. While the construction of the Sumba dolmens differs from the Caucasus, the dimensions of the plates in the structures are comparable. It should be noted that the landscape of the island is also comparable to the foothills of the Caucasus. It takes a few days for a group of Indonesians to move a multiton block several hundred meters without using machinery or animals (Figure 77). Until recently, such transportation was part of a ritual in which the use of draft animals or machinery was prohibited, and the human factor is a tribute to the tribesmen for whom the dolmen was built.[4]

As we have seen, it was possible for dolmen builders to move construction blocks, as it was done in other parts of the world. Of course, transferring megalith blocks using this method requires good roads, and archaeologists have been unable to find traces of any roads on which to transport megalithic stones.

Balance Method

As Graham Hancock points out in his book *The Sign and the Seal*:

> According to John Anthony West, an experienced Egyptologist, the Pharaohs and priests were preoccupied with a principle known as *Ma'at* often translated as "equilibrium" or "balance." It was possible, he suggested, that this principle might have been carried over into practical spheres and "that the Egyptians understood and used techniques of mechanical balance unknown to us." Such techniques would have enabled them to "manipulate these immense stones with ease and finesse.... What would be magic to us was method to them."[5]

This method makes sense if we remember what Archimedes said: Give me a place to stand and with a lever I will move the whole world.[6]

Vajra

Another interesting hypothesis is that ancient builders of dolmens carved and moved huge blocks with the help of the *vajra*, an ancient weapon (Figure 78). *Vajra* is a Sanskrit word that means "the hard or mighty one" or "thunderbolt."[7] In Indian mythology, the vajra is the powerful weapon of the god Indra, who can kill without missing. At the same time, like a diamond, it remains undestroyed in all situations: when it destroys everything, there is no scratch on it.

Probably later a "three-dimensional" vajra was replaced with a "flat" trident image. Both the vajra and the trident (*trishula*) were weapons of Lord Shiva in Hindu mythology.

The trident and the vajra are weapons of choice for many ancient gods. In Greece, this is Zeus (Jupiter in Roman mythology) and Poseidon (Neptune in Roman mythology); in South American pre-Columbian culture, it is the Aztec gods Tlaloc and Chalchiuhtlicue; in Mesopotamia, it is Marduk and Hadad (Figure 79).

Figure 78. "Opened" vajra, top, and "closed" vajra, bottom.

Figure 79. Left to right: Sumerian god Adad; Aztec god Tlaloc; modern Ukrainian coat of arms, allegedly based on the trident of Perun, the Slovenian god of thunder.

Gods pictured with the vajra were associated with both destruction and creation. According to several accounts, the vajra was used not only as a weapon of mass destruction but also as a tool for creation, that is, to cut and move megalithic blocks for constructing ancient buildings and monuments.

One such account of the vajra being used for moving megalithic blocks is known from the report of Yakov Blyumkin (Figure 80), an officer of the OGPU (Russian predecessor of the KGB).

Blyumkin has a very interesting biography that is beyond the scope of this book. However, I want to mention his account of an expedition searching for the legendary country of Shambhala (a mythical land in Tibetan Buddhism). Blyumkin's report on the expedition is still clas-

Figure 80. Yakov Blyumkin

sified. However, the Russian UFO Research Station revealed previously classified documents about this expedition. The most valuable in the case (protocol of interrogation) is Blyumkin's own testimony, in which he describes what he saw in the underground storage of Tibetan knowledge.

The note describes in detail how he went with 13 monks through a chain of underground labyrinths with a complex system of locks. To open each door, the monks each stood in a specific place, and in a process of roll-calling they dragged metal rings hanging from the ceiling on chains. Only after this did the door open with a crash. Monks showed him two secret halls that contained mechanisms of the gods. One of them had a machine that the monks called "vajra." Outwardly, it was a huge forceps, which, according to the monks, was found in underground tunnels from 8 to 10 thousand years BC. With the help of this machine, the ancient inhabitants moved huge stone blocks, although the technology of how it was done did not survive. The Hindus also used the vajra's power in construction. According to the Hindu monks, it allowed the ancient builders to move gigantic monolithic blocks of rock in the air as well as to cut up blocks of stone and rock and erect the monuments and historical structures that stand today.

Figure 81. Left to right: royal crown in the "closed" vajra style, royal crown in the "open" vajra style, dome of the St. Peter's Basilica as a "closed" vajra.

Figure 82. Are the Star of David (the Shield of David, or the five-pointed star) (left and right) and the French fleur-de-lis (center) stylized vajra?

Today one can see the vajra, the sign of supreme power, in other symbols and objects, such as royal crowns and church domes (Figures 81 and 82).

If ancient dolmen builders had access to the vajra (as many other megaliths builders around the world) that may explain how they erected dolmens in the mountains.

How the Blocks Were Lifted

A s we have seen in the previous chapters, the cover plate of a
typical dolmen could weigh between 15 and 30 metric tons and
other blocks between 3 and 8 metric tons. The average size of a
North Caucasus dolmen is 3 m (9.8 ft.) long, 2 m (6.5 ft.) wide, and 2 m
(6.5 ft.) high. How did dolmen builders put them together?

Ramps and Belts

Even as early as 1762, M. Muzar questioned legends that existed in
countries around the world about giant people who created stone structures. A hundred years later, Frederick VII, the King of Denmark, who
was also an archaeologist, believed that the construction of megaliths
did not require special means but only wooden wedges, levers, wooden
rollers, leather riggings (belts), long beams (girders), and, possibly, animals for draft power.[1]

With the help of wooden wedges and levers, it was possible to lift a
block a foot at one end, lay a stone, raise it from the other end, and use
rafters. Then, it was necessary to wrap the block with tackles and pull it
using the combined forces of people or animals. The levers helped the
movement uphill, and the wedges prevented sliding back due to gravity,
providing rest to the workforce. Moving blocks in the winter (where the
winter was cold enough) was greatly facilitated, as the hard ground and

ice allowed them to do all this without the rollers, using a girder like sleigh runners. Ramps were created to move a block up to the top of a structure.

In 1955, Norwegian ethnographer Thor Heyerdahl led an experiment on Easter Island where he and 180 men tried to erect a 13-foot (3.9 m), 10-ton Moai, a monolithic figure of a human shape, on a tree trunk and drag it. Heyerdahl was able to prove that this was possible, however, his theory about how ancient people constructed the monoliths did not satisfy everyone.

Maybe dolmens were constructed using the ramps and belts method (Figure 83, left). Local historians, keen on researching dolmens, volunteered for an hour, and without special training, lifted the lid of a dolmen 30 cm (11.8 in.) off the ground (Figure 83, right). They did this using five four-meter stakes as levers and laying stones under the slab to fix the results of each lifting attempt.

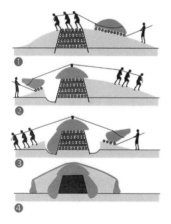 

Figure 83. Suggested steps for dolmen-building technology using ramps, left; volunteers lifted a dolmen lid 30 cm (11.8 in.) off the ground, right.

Moving Blocks Using Acoustics

Some researchers believe that in building megalithic structures a special technology was used to lift multiton stone blocks into the air with the help of special sound vibrations, or mantras. Correctly spoken, the mantras can create an energy field that, with certain skills, can move any object.

Opera singers who can potentially shatter glass by producing the correct sound loudly enough have demonstrated the power of sound. Presumably, this effect was already understood in the Old Testament, in the story that tells how trumpets were used to shatter the walls of Jericho.

This technology was known in several parts of the world. Theodore Illion, in his book *In Secret Tibet*, tells how he witnessed Tibetan monks levitating stones using acoustics.[2] The Aymara Indians of South America related to a Spanish traveler during the Spanish Conquest that its earliest inhabitants possessed supernatural powers that miraculously allowed them to lift stones off the ground and carry them through the air using the sound of a trumpet.[3]

Mayan legends say that the temple of Uxmal in Mexico was built by a race of dwarfs, who only had to whistle to move heavy rocks. It is said that if a person stands at the base of the pyramid-like Temple of the Magician and claps their hands, the stone structure at the top produces a "chirping sound."[4]

According to the ancient Greeks, the walls of Thebes were constructed by Amphion, the son of Jupiter, by moving large stones to the sound of a lyre or harp. Apollonius Rhodius recounted in the third century BC how Amphion would "sing loud and clear on his golden lyre" as "rock twice as large followed his footsteps."[5] Phoenician historian Sanchuniathon spoke of the god Ouranos founding the first city, Byblos, stating that Ouranos "devised Baetulia, contriving stones that moved as having life."[6]

Modern science describes this phenomenon as "acoustic levitation," a process that takes advantage of the properties of sound to cause solids, liquids, and heavy gases to float and which can occur in either normal or reduced gravity. Japanese scientists have been successful in moving an object in three-dimensional space using a complex system of acoustic levitation, surpassing previous research endeavors that lifted objects in two dimensions. In order to move particles, the Japanese scientists placed objects inside a complex setup of four arrays of speakers.[7]

In the past, researchers at Northwestern Polytechnical University in Xi'an, China, used ultrasound fields to successfully levitate globs of the heaviest solid and liquid—iridium and mercury, respectively. The aim of their work was to learn how to manufacture products without the aid of containers, as some compounds are too corrosive for containers to hold, or they react with containers in undesirable ways.

The Chinese scientists employed an ultrasound emitter and reflector that generated a sound pressure field. The emitter produced roughly 20-mm wavelength sounds that, in theory, could levitate objects half that wavelength or less.[8]

D. H. Childress reports in his book *Anti-Gravity and the World Grid* about a Swedish Dr. Jarl who witnessed how Tibetan monks built a rock wall by playing musical instruments, singing, and chanting prayers. Monks beat drums of various sizes, slowly increasing the sound. After some time, the big blocks of stone started to sway, took off into the air in the direction of the rock wall, and landed correctly into a predefined position on the wall.[9]

There is a strong association between areas that produce a strong resonance and the location of construction. In the mountains, sound can produce an avalanche. Since dolmens are located in mountains, it is possible that ancient builders used sound to move blocks up to the dolmen location. With the numerous reports of acoustic levitation, we can assume that it has been scientifically proven that sound can be used to move objects.

Telluric Energy

According to H. P. Blavatsky, "It is the blood of the Earth, the electro-magnetic current, which circulates through all the arteries, and which is said to be found stored in the 'navel' of the Earth."[10] In my opinion, this method is more likely to have been used by ancient dolmen builders. It was "rediscovered" several times by various researchers, as we shall see, even in modern times.

Earth (telluric) energy was known to operate, among other things, flying "machines," as well as move huge stone blocks, and even power "ordinary" cars. The complete theory of how and why telluric energy works is complex and is beyond the scope of this book.

This book has previously discussed that megaliths generate high-frequency vibrations and electromagnetic waves. Their activity increases at sunrise and sunset and intensifies during the spring and autumn equinoxes. This is because the quartz crystals in the dolmen stones are capable of converting mechanical energy into electrical energy and vice versa. Quartz, working in a huge range of frequencies, creates acoustic and electric waves due to earthquakes, volcanic eruptions, tectonic block movement, and the tidal influences of the sun, moon and other planets.

Physicists began experimenting with telluric energy in the late 19th century, the most famous being Nikola Tesla. According to free-energy researcher Patrick J. Kelly, Tesla's Dynamic Theory of Gravity of 1937 (however, never published) states that all bodies emit microwaves whose voltage and frequency are determined by their electrical contents and relative motion. Tesla measured the microwave radiation of the earth as being only a few centimeters in wavelength. He said that the frequency and voltage were influenced by the velocity and mass of the earth, and that its gravitational interaction with other bodies, such as the sun, was determined by the interaction of the microwaves between the two bodies.[11]

This produces a driving force by pushing against the space-time continuum. In November 2005, Boris Volfson was granted a patent on the space-time field concept. The important thing about this patent is not whether it presents a realistic mechanism for a practical space drive, but the fact that the US Patent Office granted the patent after what presumably was careful consideration.[12]

Tesla, followed by other scientists in the 20th century, discovered the principle of propulsion using strong electromagnetic fields. It's not about traveling on the ground, but from the ground up, with extraordinary speed and ease.

Kelly states that Tesla's experiment with high-voltage, high-frequency alternating current with a pair of parallel metal plates revealed that the "space" between the plates became what he called "solid-state," having the attributes of mass, inertia, and momentum. That showed that this area became tangible. Even mechanical push could be applied against this tangible area. After several other experiments, Tesla concluded that powerful electromagnetic waves could be used to push and pull against the "empty space." This principle, based on the Hall effect used in semiconductor magnetic sensors, is today called the magnetohydrodynamic effect. Tesla also deduced that this "empty space" actually contained:

- Independent carriers that permeate all space and all matter and from which all matter is made. These carry momentum, magnetism, electricity or electromagnetic force, and can be manipulated artificially or by nature.
- "Primary Solar Rays" (starlight), which travel at the speed of light, having frequencies far above X-rays, gamma, and UV radiation.
- "Cosmic Rays," particles in space propelled by the Primary Solar Rays.
- X-rays, gamma rays, and UV electromagnetic waves, all of which travel at the speed of light.
- Ordinary visible and infrared electromagnetic waves that travel at the speed of light.
- Rapidly varying electrostatic forces of enormous potential, emanating from the earth and other gravitational bodies in space.[13]

Most megaliths around the world, as well as many dolmens, are constructed of sandstone, a stone containing high concentrations of energy-responsive quartz crystal. Because of its crystalline structure, quartz can convert the earth's natural electrical vibrations into usable energy through a property known as piezoelectricity.

The beginning of this chapter quoted Blavatsky, as she famously said that the electromagnetic current circulates through the earth, forming some sort of grid (earth "arterias"). Many ancient monuments were built on this grid. The alignment of ancient megaliths built along the earth's electromagnetic grid is called *ley lines*. There is a theory that the megalithic system utilized the telluric energy of ley lines. According to researchers like Peter Champoux, the ancient world used a highly developed earth energy transmission system. This system harnessed and utilized transmission leys, storage containers, control centers, and receiver stations. Tools of megalithic culture and telluric management included standing stones, layered mounds, dolmens, calendar circles, and human-built building structures.

Crystals are an essential tool and technology for transmitting energy, as they take energy in one state and convert it to another state. Ancient astronaut theorists believe that early cultures that erected obelisks had some understanding of the high-tech properties of quartz and that they might have used them to transmit this energy over vast distances.

The Great Pyramid in Egypt contains large amounts of quartz crystal; therefore, it could be that the Great Pyramid, together with megaliths around the world, made up a global network of free energy. Were dolmens a part of this network?

Tesla rediscovered this method and used it to transmit energy (read, electricity) through the air. Telluric energy, together with the energy from other celestial bodies, forms a "united" cosmic energy that pervades everything. This cosmic energy, called *prana* in Indian philosophy, is "utilized" by Indian yoga adepts using pranayama breath techniques. Chinese Taoists use "breathing cosmic energy" as well to increase ones chi (qi), the vital force of any living thing.

Technology for transferring energy "by air" is available today. You may even buy a device that uses this technology in most electronic stores. Wireless charging for your cellphone is based on the principle of magnetic resonance, or inductive power transfer (IPT). This is the process of transferring an electrical current between two objects through the use of coils to induce an electromagnetic field.

The earth's electromagnetic field was probably a driving force of the *vimana*, an ancient flying machine that was described in the Indian epic poem *Mahabharata* as long ago as 4000 BC. There are also legends that King Solomon had a vimana that flew silently and fast.

Slavic folklore also references the vimana in stories about Baba Yaga, an old woman who owns magical objects and is endowed with magical power. In the tales, she flies around in a vimana-looking mortar and drives on a broom (Figure 84).

Another person who allegedly rediscovered this method and put it into practice was Latvian-born Edward Leedskalnin, who quarried and sculptured multiton limestone blocks in the 1920s (Figure 85). At Coral Castle, the limestone structure he created in Florida, Leedskalnin apparently left behind copper wires and electrical coils after the castle construction. A guide at Coral Castle indicated that Leedskalnin used to move all his stones using these wires and coils, and explained that Leedskalnin had discovered the ancient Egyptian method of using the electromagnetic earth field to move monolithic stones.

Whether dolmen builders used this method or not, we can see that other megalithic monuments were possibly constructed with the help of electromagnetic power.

Figure 84. Baba Yaga flying in a mortar.

Figure 85. Edward Leedskalnin on the cover of his book. Coral Castle is in the background.

Etheric Vapor

If ancient builders used none of the above technologies, then perhaps they used some other method now lost to history. Maybe they received all the necessary energy from water? Dowsing is known to locate water at great depths inside the earth, and there is a connection between human mental power and water. As Japanese scientist Masaru Emoto discovered in 1994, water may transmit human emotions and behave accordingly. His book *Messages from Water, Vol. 1*[14] included many pictures of beautifully shaped water crystals that were created after playing quality music, offering prayers, and speaking pleasant words to the water. At the same time, water produced "ugly" crystals in the opposite situation. Ancient builders might have used this forgotten power to deal with large stone blocks. Perhaps this is the reason why there is a water source near every dolmen?

Nevertheless, there are many other methods that could have provided such power. These methods have been uncovered periodically, but for various reasons, are either ignored or forgotten.

For example, let's take the curious case of John Ernst Worrell Keely (Figure 86), who some people think was a greater inventor than Tesla. In 1885, Keely announced that he had invented a fundamentally new mechanism that was driven by sound vibrations. According to him, he extracted the sounds with the help of ordinary tuning forks, with the sympathetic vibrations resonating with the ether.

To understand Keely's design, imagine a copper sphere 30 cm (11.8 in.) in diameter supported by a tripod. Around the base of the

Figure 86. John Keely in front of his machine.

tripod are arranged several metal rods of different lengths and thickness that, when touched, start to vibrate. Inside the sphere itself are installed plates and resonant tubes, the arrangement of which can be changed with the help of special handles. All this Keely called a "sympathetic transmitter."

Next, a glass cylinder full of water about a meter (3.2 feet) high with a metal cover is connected to the sphere by a wire. At the bottom of the cylinder are three kilogram metal balls. Keely's goal was to prove that each of the balls, like any other material body, has its own inner melody. Keely demonstrated that when vibrating tuning forks, which he sounded with the help of his handles, one ball from the bottom of the vessel would swing up under the lid of the vessel, with the two remaining balls following.

Unfortunately, when he died in 1898, Keely took his secrets to the grave with him, although several of his models are stored in the Franklin Institute in Philadelphia and in the American Precision Museum in Windsor, Vermont.

Part II

Dolmen Mysteries, Healing, and Power

W e may not know when, by whom, and for what purpose the dolmens were built, but there is no doubt that to this today dolmens remain a mystery that fascinates many people. Many researchers tried to explain why ancient builders went to such extremes to quarry, transport, build, orient, and decorate dolmens in a very specific way. However, mainstream researchers completely ignore other dolmen mysteries, such as their undoubtful electromagnetic and even mental power and influence on the human organism. This chapter will discuss these and other enigmas and unexplained phenomena that have been attributed to the North Caucasus dolmens for centuries, ever since modern peoples discovered these mysterious structures.

Enigmas and Unexplained Phenomena

There are many curious "accompanying artifacts" that seem to not belong to a "typical dolmen." They remain unexplained and practically ignored by mainstream archaeologists, and they puzzle alternative researchers. Many contradicting theories exist for these artifacts, as they do for the dolmens themselves. In this chapter, we will explore several such mysteries.

False Entrance Enigma

The facades of some dolmens display imitations of the plug, supposedly covering the entrance (Figure 87). In fact, the entrance to the inner chamber of such dolmens is created on the back panel or the side wall. Today 53 dolmens have such false entrances. There are also dol-

Figure 87. Dolmen near Prigorodny village of the Tuapse region, left; dolmen from the "Wolf Gate," right.

mens with two false entrances (for example, a dolmen from the group "Kirova-1," and some dolmens have two "real" entrances).

False entrances are known in many ancient monuments. For example, in Axum, Ethiopia, false doors (and windows) are skillfully made in stelae (Figure 88). False doors are also found in temples and tombs across ancient Egypt.

Certain places in South America are associated with passages or doorways

Figure 88. Author in front of the false door in Axum, Ethiopia.

to another world. For example, a megalithic door located in the Hayu Marca mountain region of Peru close to Lake Titicaca.

Also called Aramu Muru, the modern name Devil's Doorway comes from Catholics after the conquest. Legend says that a long time ago, great heroes went to join their gods and passed through the gate for a glorious new life of immortality. According to a powerful, ancient prophecy passed down through the generations, people believe the doorway to be some kind of portal that will open one day and the gods will appear in their lightships.

Such doors are not alone. Similar doors are in Bolivia (Figures 89) and other places.

False entrances in dolmens usually face west or east. In Egypt, false doors always face west. This orientation of false doors (known as the "Ka doors") in Egypt is considered an imaginary passage between the world of the living and the world of the dead that allowed the Ka (an element of the soul) to pass through them. The deity or the deceased could interact with the world of the living, either by passing through the door or by receiving offerings though it.

The false door is one of the most common elements found within Egyptian tomb complexes and is also one of the most important archi-

Figure 89. Author in Bolivia in one of the false doors of El Fuerte de Samaipata (Fort Samaipata), also known simply as "El Fuerte."

tectural features found in royal and nonroyal tombs, beginning with Egypt's Old Kingdom.

Based on Egyptian tradition, false entrances in dolmens may be connected to the development of ideas about death and the afterlife. This is, of course, if we assume that dolmens were burial chambers. However, archaeologists do not confirm that because not all dolmens contained human remains.

The orientation of dolmens from west to east suggests the traditional division of human life to life and death (life is east, death is west). Were false entrances connected with beliefs in the death and rebirth of the soul? False entrances might have been used as passages to the underworld (as we've seen with false doors in South America). In this case, the "real" entrance was probably used as the way back from the underworld—rebirth!

Cap-Shaped Depressions Enigma

Sometimes a dolmen roof has numerous, small, cup-shaped depressions or holes either scattered along the surface or in short rows and circles

(Figure 90). Similar signs are also found on the sides and front slabs of dolmens. Individual stones near the dolmens can also have rings of small holes. These holes were probably made by later civilizations that worshiped the existing dolmens with burning incense or blood sacrifices. This is evidence that the dolmens were considered sacred and worshiped for generations after they were built. The people who made sacrifices to the dolmens probably felt their mighty power.

Figure 90. Cup-shaped depressions on dolmens in the areas of the Janet and Doguab Rivers, left, and the Lazarevsky City District, right.

Shapsugsky Triangle: Anomalous Zone

Area, which is located in the Abinsky District near the village of Shapsugskaya, is called the Shapsugsky Triangle and is known as the "dolmen workshop" because it contains several unfinished dolmens (Figure 91).

One of the unfinished dolmens is particularly interesting. Next to this megalith are oaks with square trunks, and people who visit this place have various "unhealthy" feelings, such as dizziness, whistling in the ears, and blood pressure surges. Could it be that the dolmen was left unfinished because the builders felt this dark power?

The Shapsugsky area has repeatedly recorded the phenomena of multiple crop circles and UFO sightings. Even encounters with the yeti are not unheard of. Shapsugsky National District is definitely one of the most interesting and mysterious places in the Krasnodar area.

Figure 91. Unfinished dolmen in the "dolmen workshop" in the Shapsugskaya anomalous zone.

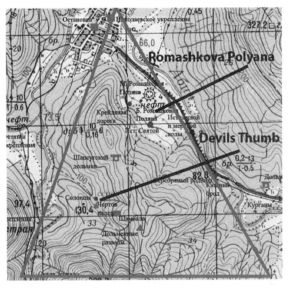

Figure 92. Map of the Shapsugsky Triangle (marked in red).

Shapsugskaya village was named for the Shapsug people who lived there. They are a subethnos of the Adyghe, one of the largest Adyghe tribes, and the Shapsug language is a dialect of the Adyghe language. The anomalous area on the map fits in one of the angles of a triangle whose sides are the river beds that start there (Figure 92). Therefore, it is called the Shapsugsky Triangle, but not only because of this but also by analogy with the famous Bermuda Triangle, another zone with unusual properties. Some consider it to be sacred, while others call it a geopathogenic zone. (The word *geopathogenic*, a combination of two Greek words, *geo* meaning "earth" and *pathos* meaning "suffering" or "disease." In ancient times these zones where considered to be godforsaken "black spots" for human well-being.) It seems that both are right.

In the middle of Romashkova Polyana ("Chamomile Meadow"), not far from Shapsugskaya village, smoke spirals from underground. This is probably because the meadow has volcanic activity and is an overthrust fault (an overthrust fault is a reverse fault in which the rocks on the upper surface of a fault plane have moved over the rocks on the lower surface). As a result of this tectonic process, more ancient layers of soil end up on top of younger ones. The difference in the age of the soils is 2.53 billion years. Tectonic activity could be one of the reasons for the anomalous phenomena: people having hallucinations, psychic insights, and clairvoyant flashes.

This area has many mineral springs that are known for their unique healing properties. A famous one, called the Silver Spring, is believed to contain living and dead water. It is located on the edge of the Romashkova Polyana, near the road that leads to the village.

The stream from the spring is divided into two (Figure 93). One spring has the living water stream (according to the legend this water brings the dead to life), the other has the dead water steam (according to the legend this water kills). The water in the spring contains a lot of silver, so it can be preserved without spoiling for a long time (up to one year). It does not dry up even during the dry season. People believe that this water is very good for the health and is capable of healing incurable diseases.

Several years ago, Silver Spring was consecrated by the Russian Orthodox Church, and now baptism rites are performed there. Despite the fact that infants are sometimes bathed in water that is –20 degrees

Figure 93. The sacred Silver Spring in the Chamomile Meadow.

Celsius (–4 degrees Fahrenheit), it is reported that none of them is sick after that.

Another energetically active place in the Shapsugsky Triangle is the Devil's Thumb (Figure 92 and 94). This is a boulder 15 m (49 ft.) high that is located on a fracture of the earth's crust and that points to the sky like a huge threatening fist. Old people say that before World War II the rock was a silhouette of a dark giant finger pointing to the sky. Later, the rock was blown up, the upper part collapsed, and the main mass was cut by a deep crack. It is unknown who destroyed this natural monument, but according to one version, it was a random German shell. Another story says that local members of the Komsomol organization did this while engaged in clearing mines (although this is unusual activity for Komsomol members).

In olden times, members of the "white brotherhood" and Satanists held their meetings near the Devil's Thumb. Even today, they may continue their rituals, as there are several sacrificial rocks in the area, and from time to time fresh blood is found on these rocks. Analysis of one of these blood samples showed that it belonged to an animal that was obviously sacrificed.

Figure 94. The Devil's Thumb in the Shapsugsky Triangle.

People who visit this place sometimes become hysterical and some even experience epileptic seizures. People say that once a congress of representatives of esoteric teachings met at the Devil's Thumb and one of the participants went into the woods and disappeared. They found him two days later in an agitated mental state.

By contrast, the Devil's Thumb has a positive impact on other visitors. One time when children with mental disabilities were brought there on a tour, they suddenly and surprisingly started asking the adults "very smart" questions that even children with normal mental abilities would not think of.

Near the Devil's Thumb are mineral springs, rich in iodine and bromine, that are more than 170 million years old. Gray-blue clay periodically erupts from the mud volcano and flows as a blue stream down into the valley. The mud contains gases that can be ignited when you put a match to its gurgling bubbles. You can put this blue mud on a sore spot and it will be healed. Before World War II, there was a spa complex

Figure 95. Grand Shapsug Dolmen, affectionately called "Grandpa."

here that offered medical procedures to patients with bone and joint diseases.

The area of the Devil's Thumb is considered to have "dark" negative power, even while the vicinity of the well-preserved Grand Shapsug Dolmen (or "Shapsugsky-1") is one of "positive" energy (Figure 95). This dolmen attracts people who believe that its energy may cure their illnesses. There are legends about the miraculous healing of many people from incurable diseases. One woman, a cancer patient, visited the dolmen and her cancer disappeared. Now she lives in a manually erected camp in the Shapsugsky Triangle from spring to autumn, returning home only for the winter. Everything in the camp is arranged for children, along with hundreds of parents, to meditate and live in the camp.

Figure 96. Tree of love.

Others believe that around the dolmen you can connect with the cosmic energy. A lot of people watching around the dolmen (and not only Shapsugskaya) see flying translucent balls. Some call them the "dead souls of the gods," while some call them "blobs of cosmic energy."

Trees around the dolmen are also considered to be "holy." One of them is called the "tree of love" (Figure 96). This is a natural "sculpture"

Figure 97. Stone plates with unusual patterns.

created by a hardwood hornbeam tree wrapping itself several times around an oak. It is believed that the "tree of love" grants wishes to people who are seeking love. Many women come there dreaming of finding a proper match or of conceiving a child. Reportedly, their dreams come true after the visit!

When hiking in this anomalous zone, you can encounter stone plates (Figure 97) with strange patterns and parts of destroyed dolmens.

In the zone also stands a pyramid-like mountain called Ostraya ("sharp") that is 630 m (2,067 ft.) high. Ostraya is considered to be a sacred mountain with strong powers itself.

While the Krasnodar Krai area has registered many anomalous zones and unusual geological and archaeological places, this book doesn't allow us to list all of these mysterious places. You may visit one of the websites (in the Russian language) to learn more about them.

Double Stars, Ancient Astronauts, and UFOs

Our story about dolmens would not be complete if we didn't discuss the dolmen connection to ancient astronauts and UFOs, as dolmens have their share in this particular area. Several dolmens display a pair of closely located dots (round projections) that ancient builders probably went to great pains to leave on the stone walls (Figures 98 and 99).

Figure 98. Dolmen in the Gelendzhik region of Russia with bas-relief and round projections.

They may represent a double star. In observational astronomy, a double star, or visual double, is a pair of stars that appear close to each other in the sky as seen from Earth when viewed through an optical telescope. This could be Mizar and Alcor: Mizar is the second star from the end of the Big Dipper's handle, and Alcor is its faint companion. Or it may even be Mintaka (Delta Orionis or 34 Orionis), a double star that is 915 light-years away and shines with a magnitude of 2.21. Mintaka is 90,000 times more luminous than the sun, and the two stars orbit each other every 5.73 days.

Figure 99. Dolmen in the Bol'shoye Pseushkho area of Tuapse.

Beta (b) Orionis, better known as Rigel, is one of the brightest stars in the sky. A companion 1/400 as bright lies just 10 arc seconds to its south, creating one of the most spectacular magnitude-contrast pairs in the heavens. Note that these stars cannot be seen by the naked eye.

Sirius, or Alpha Canis Majoris, is one of the most fascinating and challenging doubles in the sky. The primary star is the brightest and second closest of all the naked-eye stars, and its faint companion is the nearest white dwarf to Earth.

From the Pyramid Texts, which are among the oldest religious writings in the world, we know that the ancient Egyptians believed that the gods descended from the belt of Orion and from Sirius (the brightest star in the sky) in the form of human beings. Orion was associated with the god Osiris, and Sirius was associated with the goddess Isis, who together, according to ancient Egyptian wisdom, created all of human civilization.

Is it possible that these double dots on dolmen walls represented the stars Orion and Sirius? According to mainstream archaeologists, dolmens were built at the same time as the Egyptian pyramids. As we have previously seen, dolmens have similar construction elements as other megaliths, including structures in Egypt. Therefore, the people who built them may have the same beliefs about the ancient Egyptian gods Osiris and Isis.

Of course, these "dots" could also be the sun or moon rising and setting over a day. In this connection, I remember a theory about Nemesis, the mystical companion of the sun. Research indicates that, theoretically, Nemesis is a dwarf star thought to be a companion to our sun.[1] This theory was postulated to explain a perceived cycle of mass extinctions in Earth's history. In the early 1980s, scientists noticed that extinctions on Earth seemed to fall in a cyclical pattern, with mass extinctions occurring about every 27 million years. The long span of time caused them to turn to astronomical events for an explanation.

Scientists speculated that such a star could affect the orbit of objects in the far outer solar system, sending them on a collision course with Earth. While recent astronomical surveys failed to find any evidence that such a star exists, a 2017 study suggests that a "Nemesis" may have existed in the ancient past.

One more interesting possibility is that these pairs of "dots" found on several dolmens may represent a planet Nibiru, or Planet X, or simply a 12th planet that exists beyond Pluto. Nibiru in the ancient Akkadian language means "crossing." The Akkadians considered Nibiru the seat of the god who shepherds the stars like sheep; the Babylonians identified it with the god Marduk, and the Sumerians also knew of this planet.

This planet, unlike the other planets in our solar system, has an elliptical orbit and moves clockwise rather than counterclockwise. It is believed that Earth was created after Nibiru collided with another planet, Maldek, in our solar system.

Soviet-born Sumerian cuneiform translator and ancient astronaut proponent Zecharia Sitchin argues that Nibiru passes through our solar system every 3,600 years. According to Sitchin, this planet is inhabited by the Anunnaki (the Nephilim, or biblical race of giants), "those who from heaven to Earth came." They landed on Earth, colonized it, mined the earth for gold and other minerals, established a spaceport in the Iraq-Iran area, and lived as a small colony in a kind of idealistic society. They returned when Earth was more populated and genetically modified human DNA to create a slave race to work their mines, farms, and other enterprises in Sumeria, the so-called "cradle of civilization" taught in school history texts. They created modern humans, Homo sapiens, through genetic manipulation of their DNA with the hominid Homo erectus.[2]

Perhaps in the past, people noticed Nibiru when it was close to Earth (as it passed through our solar system every 3,600 years), and was a fact definitely worth commemorating.

Another interesting connection is between dolmens and UFOs. For example, on the portal plates of the Shapsugsky and Aderbievsky dolmens are drawings of the terrain with a floating device (Figure 100). These pictures depict a place with a line of mountains (horizontal triangles) and three rivers depicted with rows of zigzags. A mountain divides the last river on the right into two streams. A UFO is shown flying across the mountains. This same picture is on dolmens in two different locations! Whether this picture is actually showing a UFO or not, even today many people report seeing UFOs over dolmens.

Figure 100. Ornaments on the slabs of the Aderbievsky and Shapsugsky dolmens.[3]

Puzzles of the Dolmen Signs and Symbols

S trange signs and symbols have been found on several dolmens. Were they part of the original decoration? However, no writing of any kind has been discovered inside or outside of dolmens. Are these signs some kind of writing system of the mysterious dolmen builders? Whatever it is, we can only guess, as it has yet to be deciphered.

Phosphenes

Of course, there could be another explanation for the geometrical patterns found on dolmens (Figure 100). Prototypes of those elementary symbols found on dolmens could be phosphenes, which are subjective images that do not depend on external light (Figure 101). The word *phosphene* comes from the Greek words *phos* (light) and *phainein* (to show).[1] It is a phenomenon characterized by the experience of seeing light without light actually entering the eye and are visual sensations that are the result of internal processes occurring in the human body. And because they are experienced inside the eye and the brain, they can be considered common to all humans. Sometimes phosphenes appear spontaneously, especially if the person has been deprived of visual stimuli for some time. They can also be experienced by external stimuli: pressure on the eyeball, a sudden shock, or attempting to peer into the darkness immediately after awakening.

The same effect can be achieved through a number of chemicals. It has long been known that phosphenes in the form of abstract motifs are a direct result of the use of hallucinogens such as LSD, psilocybin, mescaline, harmaline, and bufotenine. Moreover, for people of different cultures, these images are the same. Because they are the same in different parts of the world, they can't be ascribed to mere coincidence. And depending on the cultural context, they are assigned special significance. At the same time, people can see similar images even months after the experience. It is possible that the ancient dolmen builders, while in an altered state of consciousness, saw the images, which were then depicted on the dolmens where these images were observed.

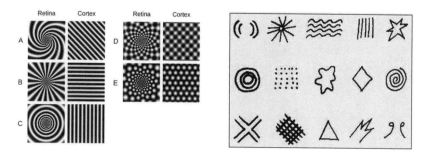

Figure 101. Phosphenes observed inside the human visual cortex and eyes, left;[2] 15 of the most common images of phosphenes, right.[3]

Suzanne Carr, in her work *Entoptic Phenomena*, mentions that, according to G. Oster "seeing stars" is seeing phosphenes, an experience that can be induced by a blow on the head or other mechanical means.[4] A less violent procedure is to apply gentle pressure to the eyeballs with the fingers with the eyes closed to cause a phosphene to appear: a glowing circle or part of a circle, apparently about a quarter of an inch in diameter. The phosphene's location in the visual field is opposite the point the finger touches, at the outer edge of the field when the eyelid is touched near the nose, and low in the field when the center of the upper lid is touched. J. Walker discusses this in more detail when describing all the methods by which phosphenes can be generated through pressure alone.[5]

Whether images on the dolmens were phosphenes or rivers with mountains, they were made at the time of the dolmen construction. Dolmen builders went to great lengths to "carve" them on the walls. However, other images that were "etched" on the walls were made after the dolmen was finished and were probably not by the original builders.

Petroglyphs

Some dolmens have petroglyphs etched on the walls (Figures 102 and 103). These petroglyphs can be evidence that dolmens were built before the "petroglyph era" (that is, before the Great Flood).

Figure 102. East of Gelendzhik, six km (3.7 mi.) from the city center, is the two-headed Mount Nexis with the "moon" dolmen.

Note that petroglyphs (as well as *tamgas* and runes, discussed in the next sections) are etched into the surface of the dolmen and do not stand out on the surface. Because of the different techniques used to

Figure 103. Dolmen in Dzhubga village with petroglyphs, left; drawings of the petroglyphs, right.

produce them, this is evidence that they were made after the dolmen was finished and probably not by the original builders.

Dolmens and Tamgas

Several petroglyphs found on dolmens resemble *tamgas* (Figure 104). A tamga, or tamgha, is an abstract seal or stamp, usually the emblem of a particular tribe, clan, or family. They were common among Eurasian nomads throughout classical antiquity and the Middle Ages (Figure 105). Similar "tamga-like" symbols were sometimes adopted by peoples adjacent to the Pontic-Caspian steppe, both in Eastern Europe and Central Asia. Archaeologists prize tamgas as a first-rate source for the study of present and extinct cultures. Usually, a descendant of a certain tribe borrowed his ancestor's tamga and added an additional element or modified it.

Figure 104. Dolmen Hamyshki-1, resembling a tamga, or seal.

Figure 105. Examples of Adyghe tamgas.

There are several cases of combining two or even three tamgas in the same group, that could indicate the image of kinship, friendships, or other close ties (marriage, twinning, fosterage, reconciliation of blood feud enemies, etc.). G. F. Turchaninov, in his book *The Discovery and Deciphering of the Ancient Writing of the Caucasus*, deciphered one group of five characters of syllabi-hieroglyphic type as writing that the Circassians used up to the 17th century.

It is possible that when the Adyghe people "discovered" dolmens and learned that dolmens were "places of power," they "claimed" them as their clans.

Dolmens and Runes

In popular culture, runes have always been seen as possessing mystical properties. Modern Wiccan sects use runes ceremonially and ritualistically. Runes date from before the Christianization of Northern Europe and became associated with the "pagan" or non-Christian past, and hence a mystique is cast upon them.[6] Even the supposed etymology of the word *rune*, the Old High German word *rūnēn*, which means "to whisper," helped to add a secretive bent to runes.[7] The first runic inscriptions that have survived to the modern day date from the second century AD. The runic alphabet consists of 24 letters—18 consonants and six vowels (Figure 106):

ᚠ	ᚢ	ᚦ	ᚠ	ᚱ	ᚲ	ᚷ	ᚹ
f	u	þ	a	r	k	g	w
/f/	/u/	/þ/	/a/	/r/	/k/	/g/	/w/

ᚺ	ᚾ	ᛁ	ᛃ	ᛇ	ᛈ	ᛉ	ᛊ
h	n	i	j	ï	p	z(ʀ)	s
/h/	/n/	/i/	/j/	/i/	/p/	/z/	/s/

ᛏ	ᛒ	ᛖ	ᛗ	ᛚ	ᛜ	ᛞ	ᛟ
t	b	e	m	l	ŋ	d	o
/t/	/b/	/e/	/m/	/l/	/ng/	/d/	/o/

Figure 106. The runic alphabet known as the Futhark (Futhark is the Scandinavian name for the runic alphabet. There are various futharks, the Elder Futhark being the oldest).[8]

The runic alphabet is known as the Futhark, a name composed from the first six letters of the alphabet, namely f, u, th, a, r, and k. In this way, *Futhark* is analogous to the word *alphabet*, which is from alpha and beta, the first two letters of the Greek alphabet. No one knows why the letters were ordered in this way, but it might be some form of mnemonic function that was not preserved. These runes have been found on a dolmen located in Mamedovo Gorge (Lazarevskoye Microdistrict) (Figure 107).

Note the similarities with the Futhark runes (Figure 106). However, this similarity doesn't explain the main question of who built the dolmens and why!

Figure 107. Runes on a dolmen in Mamedovo Gorge, left, and a drawing of the runes, right.

Mysterious Artifacts and Geological Formations

S
trange artifacts and unusual geological formations are often found in the areas where dolmens stand. Whether these artifacts are associated with dolmens is not clear. Besides the Shapsugsky Anomalous Zone (see the previous chapter), unusual geological formations found in the same area may be products of the dolmen's mysterious power (see "Progress-Boosting Technology and Baby-Making Machine" and "Dolmen Power" for more information). Whatever the reason for the artifacts and formations discussed in this book, in my personal opinion, connections between the artifacts and the dolmens are possible. However, we are not aware today of such connections. Maybe because we don't know for sure the answers to the questions raised in the previous chapters: who, when, how (quarry and transport), and why (such a particular shape); more importantly, what was the purpose of building these ancient structures.

Stone Gears

How can one explain the artifacts of unknown purpose that we see in Figure 108? Are they details of an incomprehensible prehistoric mechanism? Some people argue that they belong to ancient mill, however, it has not been confirmed that a mill existed so high in the mountains and far from a water source.

Figure 108. Mysterious megaliths found among dolmens.

Stone Mushrooms

In the village of Noviy in the Abinsky District, at an altitude of 125 m (410 ft.) above sea level, a network of dolmens exists. The population of this small village is only 900 and it exists only thanks to the rather gloomy establishments located here: prisons, a penal colony, a madhouse, and a military unit, whose duties include protecting all these establishments. The location of these facilities may have been purposely chosen. The area has many dolmens, and the dolmen power may influence the "correction" of the imprisoned individuals. We will learn more about dolmen power later in the book.

However, some rather unusual formations called "stone mushrooms" are located here (Figure 109).

Figure 109. Geological formation in the shape of mushroom.

These "mushrooms" are positioned in the forest, where there is no strong wind or water. How were these "mushrooms" formed in the first place? Similar structures exist in other places, but they are always the work of wind or water.

Cult Stone with Seats

The "cult stone with seats" is located near the village of Kudepsta in Sochi (Figure 110).

Figure 110. This megalith with two "seats" is located in the Kudepsta micro-district.

M. Kudin, in his article "Calendar Motifs in Dolmen Culture," argues that the closest analogies to this stone are the rock sanctuaries of Thrace and Phrygia dedicated to the goddess Cybele, which in Phrygian means "mountain."[1] The seats of the Kudepstan stone are almost identical to the "Pelop's throne" on the top of the Sipylus mountain (Turkey).

In 1966, the famous ethnographer Sh. Inal-Ipa examined and described the Kudepstan sacrificial stone.[2] It is a block of gray-yellow sandstone up to 5 m (16.4 ft.) long, about 4.5 m (14.8 ft.) wide, and about 1.5 m (3.2 ft.) high. The anterior, northeastern part of the rock has two cavities in the form of seats, 45 cm (17.7 in.) deep and 75 cm (29.5 in.)

wide, divided by a common "armrest." Behind the seats, in the upper plane of the stone, is a sarcophagus-like depression 1.95 m (6.4 ft.) long and up to 0.90 m (3 ft.) wide. This "sarcophagus," with the head elevated in the southeastern part, may have been edged with a rim, but today appears destroyed from the side of the seats. On the preserved upper part of the rim are several small, cup-shaped cavities.

Together with V. Orlkinym, Sh. Inal-Ipa excavated near the stone.[3] In front of the seats they found a pavement of large sandstone slabs with an area of about 3 m (9.8 ft.). At the northeastern edge of the pavement, on a large circular plate, a hearth was located opposite the center of the seats. Also, about 7 m (23 ft.) to the northeast, they found a second hearth composed of four large stone blocks.

Sh. Inal-Ipa was inclined to attribute the sacrificial stone to the late Middle Ages, but such authoritative archaeologists as U. Voronov and V. Markovin placed this monument during the time of the dolmen construction.[4] Indeed, the manner of manufacturing the stone allows us to consider that this monument belongs to the time of the dolmens. Indirectly, this confirms the location of the monument. Its seats have a 60-degree azimuth and mark the sunrise over the mountain slope on the day of the summer solstice. The facades of dolmens often mark this important astronomical direction as well. Thanks to excavations, it was found that in this case the reference line of the solstice formed by the hearths also emphasizes the direction of the solstice.

Kurgan Artifacts

Kurgan is a Slavic word for "burial mound," which is really an earth pyramid, or barrow (Figure 111).

There were many kurgans in Russia where I used to live. Some of them have been excavated and the artifacts are now displayed in various museums. Besides figurines made of gold and jewelry, pretty curios have also been found (Figures 112 and 113). What exactly were ancient peoples trying to symbolize by creating these figures?

Figure 111. View of a Scythian Alexandropol kurgan dated 394–366 BC, before excavation in 1852–1856.[5]

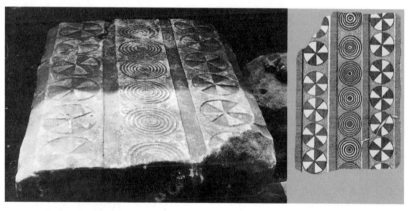

Figure 112. Findings from kurgan (barrow) number 11, also called Kurgan Serebrajnuyj (silver).

Similar motifs of concentric circles and double spirals exist in other parts of the world. One can find examples of these patterns in New-grange in Ireland (Figure 114).

The spiral symbolizes the continuous movement of the sun and as well as duality: sunrise and sunset, beginning and end, coming and

Figure 113. Plate from Kurgan Serebrajnuyj.

Figure 114. Stone with double spirals in the Newgrange, Ireland, left; ancient symbol of yin and yang, right.

Figure 115. Mysterious column of unknown origin, left, and a large round stone plate, right, found in one of the kurgans, Klady 2 ("the Treasure 2").

going, birth and death, emergence and dying. The spiral has no beginning and no end; it is an image of birth and water, waves, movements, top and bottom, sky and underground, yin and yang (Figure 114).

Other unusual and unexplained artifacts have been discovered in different kurgans (Figure 115).

Maykop Slab

The so-called "Maykop slab" (Figure 116) is another mystery. In 1960, a stone with mysterious signs was found on a farm near the city of Maykop in the Adygea Republic. The stone would have remained hidden in a vault with other archaeological materials, but in 1963 it was accidentally "discovered" by L. Lavrov, an ethnographer and expert on the epigraphy of the Caucasus. He took the slab to Leningrad and showed it to the leading Soviet experts on ancient writings. Several attempts were made to decipher the stone, and although it has not been completely deciphered, two variations of the inscription exist.

Professor G. F. Turchaninov from the Institute of Linguistics of the USSR Academy of Sciences compared the signs on the plate with biblical pseudo-hieroglyphic letters and found that some elements reminded him of Hittite hieroglyphics.

Figure 116. The "Maykop slab" with unusual symbols.

According to paleographic features, Turchaninov dated the inscription to the 13th and 12th centuries BC and considered it a work of the Colchis, who once lived along the coast of the Black Sea. But the most surprising thing to Turchaninov was that the inscription was easy to read in Abkhazian; it described the city of Ayia, owned by a local ruler and built somewhere in the foothills. According to Turchaninov, the inscription reads: "This

Azeg king of the Great Marna is a descendant (son). Fortress Aya is his property. Pagya from Khiza came here at the beginning of the month of the sowing in the year 21, built this fortress in the country of rocks, in a gold-bearing land, in Valley of Pahu."[6]

Turchaninov connected this inscription with the myth of the Argonauts. He wrote about possible contacts between the ancient Abkhazians and the Phoenicians and Hittites, and he even identified the ancient Sindi people who lived on the Taman Peninsula with the Abkhazians. As for the ancient city mentioned in the inscription, he assumed that it once stood in the valley of the White River, in the territory of Adygea.

Another scholar, archaeologist N. Lovpache, compared the Maykop plate with inscriptions on Maeotian tablets from the later Maeotian culture, inscriptions that, so far, have eluded any decoding. He also published his translation of the Maykop text using the reconstruction of the old Adyghe language: "Gasutava is the priest of god Hebatu, a 50-year-old man completed the construction of the city, after he came to the area 'Gardens,' for the son of the royal house of Soupule—the younger brother of the king Arnuvandy. A thousand hands (builders) he delivered, stone and hornbeam in city. In the 25th year of prosperity in his seventh month, the ruler consecrated the palace fortress 'Ma-e' in honor of the female deity Hayama (Najama), by the 21st sacrificial sheep and the plough (ard plough or scratch plough) ploughed."[7]

Today, this stone is a part of the Kunstkamera Museum collection in St. Petersburg and still remains undeciphered.

Mahoshkushha Petroglyphs

Other interesting artifacts are the Mahoshkushha petroglyphs (Figure 117), which are engraved stones uncovered in the Republic of Adygea by local students, who discovered these stones in 1983 in a gravel pit at Mahoshkushha Mountain, east of Maykop. These petroglyphs, about 90 of which have been found, may date to the ninth century BC and are still undeciphered.

Figure 117. Some of the Mahoshkushha petroglyphs showing the image of a prehistoric elephant, mastodon, or mammoth.[8]

One can see two types of human figures on the stones. The torsos of some figures are elongated while others are short. Another Mahoshkushha stone depicts a seven-pointed "star of Tlepsh," the Adyghe god of iron and forge-craft, who fashioned an arrow meant to kill only certain people. This Nart legend, depicted on one of the Mahoshkushha stones, says that the arrow was intended for three people: Sosruko, Psh"jetyk"kIjekI (short-necked), and Blypk"kIjekI (with short body). The magic arrow did not stop until it struck the person whose name the shooter said before launching the arrow. Psh"jetyk"kIjekI and Blypk"kIjekI were killed, but Sosruko managed to outsmart the arrow of Tlepsh and survive by turning himself into clay and clinging to the foot of the mountain.[9]

These engraved stones remind me of the Ica stones—engraved stones found in the Ica Province of Peru. Unfortunately, archaeologists do not take the Ica stones seriously because drawings of dinosaurs appear together with humans on the stones. By contrast, the Mahoshkushha petroglyphs enjoy serious study by local historians and archaeologists.

Urushten Idols

The idols of Urushten are a group of rocks and large stones that remotely resemble humans or animals (Figure 118). Some of the sculptures have petroglyphs in the form of tamgas, cup-shaped signs, lines, or wide grooves. These rocks are located in the interfluve of the Malaya, Laba, and Urushten Rivers, at the end of Shahgireevsky gorge in the Mostovsky district of the Krasnodar region.

Figure 118. "Idols" in the form of a human head with a face.

If the "idols" are not on the rock, they are stand-alone sculptures on boulders of serpentinite that are 3 m (9.85 ft.) or larger. People notice different sculptures resembling a bison, a hippo (a prehistoric hippo that once lived in Europe?), a bear, a wild boar, a fox, a turtle, a deer, and a fish.

The Marcahuasi plateau in the Andes Mountains of Peru, not far from Lima, also has curiously shaped rocks resembling human faces and animals. Archaeologists, as in the case of the Ica stones, do not recognize the Marcahuasi statues as legitimate artifacts that require closer attention. However, Russian and Adyghe archaeologists study the Urushten idols and consider them to have historic value.

Loo's Plate

The Loo's plate (Figure 119), an archaeological monument discovered less than 20 years ago, was first seen in a ravine between the railway and highway north of the village of Loo (pronounced as 'l-aw-aw'), but it was not properly assessed and did not strike any interest until a local archaeologist rediscovered it in 2013.

Adyghe archaeologist N. Lovpache suggests that the symbols on the plate describe the soul and the afterlife; according to him, this confirms the funereal function of the North Caucasus megaliths.[10] Prior to his discovery, the most ancient literary monument was the Maykop plate, which was determined to be more then 3,000 years old. The age of the Loo's plate is 4,000 years—between the second and third millennia BC.

Figure 119. The Loo's plate.

The plate is 60 x 50 cm (23.6 x 19.7 in.) and 16–22 cm (6.3–8.7 in.) thick. It is decorated with about 50 symbols, although an accurate count is difficult because the compositions intertwine.

Most of the petroglyphs are signs or symbols found among the Hittite characters: a rectangular grid with seven parallel lines; a triangle with a hole in the center; and six- and seven-pointed stars, among others. Some symbols are recognized as a dolmen, a figure of a deer on a pole, a schematic outline of a fish, a structure with a gabled roof, or a sailing ship. According to the Adyghe people's symbolism, the "fish" personifies the underworld into which people leaving this world sail in a "solar boat," like the pharaoh in the ancient Egyptian *Book of the Dead*.

In my opinion, the images of dolmens on this stone are proof that the dolmens were built prior to the "invention" of even primitive writing. The dolmens were there before peoples with primitive sign-symbol writing came to the area.

The above examples of unusual artifacts are just a small part of the many archaeological wonders that have been discovered in the areas around the dolmens. While menhirs, megalithic complexes with temples, ruins of ancient cities, stone circles, underground structures, and other fascinating ancient monuments exist, the dolmens that proudly stand today in these difficult-to-access areas no doubt are the most mysterious "artifacts" of the whole North Caucasus.

Dolmen Power

remember the first time I touched a dolmen—I felt a strong power emanating from the stones, my head started spinning, and bright stars appeared before my closed eyes. Scared, I quickly pulled my hand away and opened my eyes.

Soviet researchers R. Furdui and U. Shvaydak hypothesized that based on the material from which dolmens are made, they serve as emitters of ultrasonic vibrations.[1] Installed in unapproachable places and "running" at a certain frequency, they did not allow enemies to enter the protected site by causing feelings of fear, loss of consciousness, and sometimes death. Even now, when approaching some of the dolmens, one can feel a strong wave action that can cause a headache and weakness.

Psychics uncovered a curious pattern about the dolmens: stones that one of them considers particularly powerful may seem completely lifeless to others. Positive and negative effects are also determined in different ways, and a person can perceive a particular stone to have different powers at different times. However, everyone who has tried to communicate with a dolmen notices an intensification in vital body processes. Often when "communicating" with a dolmen, people feel unwell, become emotionally stressed, or feel different degrees of euphoria; some even experience nervous breakdowns. Interesting results are seen when observing children. After visiting the dolmens, children suddenly begin to paint, write poetry or stories, and exhibit psychic abilities. Their character and behavior also changes dramatically, but in a positive way.

Egregore and Dolmen Power

Egregore is an occult concept that refers to a "thought form" or a "collective group mind," and is an autonomous psychic entity made up of, and influencing, the thoughts of a group of people.[1] Dolmens are well known for influencing this thought form. E. Volkova and S. Valganov, in their online publication "The Riddle of the Dolmens," describe her family's impressions from their journey to these ancient megaliths:

> Objects of my observation: I, my husband, children ranging in age from 8 to 16 years, adults of varying sex, age, profession, residence, and relationship to me.
>
> Time and conditions of observation: Two-and-a-half years of intensive trips to areas where dolmens are located. For the purity of the experiment, we did not use any techniques, practices, rituals, etc. On the contrary, we were mainly concerned with getting rid of the perceived limitations and distortions of perception.
>
> A direct but fairly impartial observation (I did not even know approximately what was needed or could be expected from dolmens—there was only a hint that some unusual reactions were possible) made it possible to reveal some general patterns of psychological human responses, which are really quite unpredictable and not the result of any physical or other form of preparation. . . . Immediately, there was a significant difference in the behavior "in the conditions of the dolmens" between children and adults. Virtually all the adults who came to the dolmens for the first time (with a small but significant exception) had an emotional outburst (and in women, some breakdowns). However, children experienced a creative upsurge.

Adults often feel around the dolmens an incomprehensible anxiety and irritation, sometimes becoming unacceptable and significantly limiting the time spent in the area of the dolmens, and often leading to eccentric behavior. Children quickly adapted to the unfamiliar environment, often discovering new, unexpected features, which surprised their parents.

I noticed a difference in behavior during the stay with the dolmens: the children experienced "ups and downs" of perception, or periodic changes of openness and closeness; adults, in general "worked themselves up" emotionally and were unable to notice, evaluate, and take control of their condition.

Any reactions occurring here are hypertrophied. In humans, those features that are hidden from consciousness elsewhere are manifested here, influencing their actions. This applies to adults and children, but the results are different, primarily in time: children, faced with the need to admit their mistakes, react quickly enough and correct their behavior accordingly; adults can, for years, deny and complain about fate, find excuses, but do not in fact change anything. This is reflected in the attitude toward me as the leader of the group: in whatever tough times one sometimes has to talk to a child, he eventually recognizes the validity of my remarks or actions and does not harbor a grudge against me, "stepping back" literally before my eyes. An adult can hold on to an unpleasant event for years, avoiding any communication, and only soften with time.

Especially I want to say about adolescence. The contradiction between the desire to look like an adult and the habits of acting like a child are also exaggerated and can lead to all sorts of conflicts. A feature of this with the dolmens is that there is a noticeable misunderstanding about the signs of adulthood, or an incorrect emphasis on external aspects. Faced with this aspect in one of the campaigns, I came to the conclusion that youthful initiation in any form is a necessary moment in the normal development of the personality.

Perhaps the main difference between adults and children at the dolmens is that the children come close to a state "as they are conceived by God," and the adults look like "how they made themselves." Based on my experience of taking groups to dolmens for several years, one can make some conclusions:

- There is a need to adjust before and during the stay with the dolmens (cleansing at all levels).
- Subjects who bring the body into a harmonious state near the dolmens go beyond their usual range of possibilities.
- Deep features of the personality appear that are mostly hidden in everyday life.
- The absence of any expectations, the ability to let go of oneself, trusting one's nature, opens the way to reality, to the unknown.
- The position and behavior of the person among the dolmens inevitably affects the quality of events that occur to them.
- There was a visible manifestation of the possibility of using collective energy.
- After trips to the dolmens, and as a result of the experience gained there, a person's habitual way of life, well-being, social relations, and eventually world view changes, sometimes in contrast to their immediate desires.[2]

Probably when people spend time among the dolmens they inadvertently apply their thoughts and expectations based on their life experience. Egregore, born of these thoughts, is able to manage human lives in a global way. These forces can be good and evil, life and death, or order and chaos. This is why it is very important to "cleanse" yourself mentally and even physically before visiting dolmens.

There are also conflicting opinions whether it is possible to protect yourself from the egregore and ask the egregore for something. To do this, it is sufficient to "tune" and "trigger the egregore" accordingly.

Some authors see them as useful and protective, while others are wary of open interaction with egregores and talk about the absolute necessity of being protected from them in everyday life.[3]

Dolmens and the Tarot

Connections with ancient megalithic sites can be seen in modern tarot cards. In ancient times, the training of priests consisted of philosophical paintings and explanatory diagrams that reflected the unity of the laws of the universe. After dedicating himself to studying, the student began to understand the integrity and harmony of the world. Becoming an ecclesiastic, he was simultaneously a painter, an architect, and a physician.

Subtle memories of this ancient system are preserved in tarot cards. Many of the cards display ancient megalithic structures, such as the Magi-

Figure 120. Major Arcana tarot cards depicting the Magician.

171

cian, a Major Arcana card that shows a magician behind a stone table (Figure 120). On the table are the symbols of the four elements of the universe: a sword, the symbol of fire and purification; a bowl, the symbol of water, life, and memory; a pentacle, the symbol of the earth and human beings; and a scepter, the symbol of the air, heaven, and controlling the world. The Magician holds a wand over his head, while his other hand points to the ground. This means that he accepts the will of the Creator, which passes through him to transform the world. A serpent—the symbol of wisdom and protection—is wrapped around his waist.

Based on this explanation, we can view a dolmen with a bas-relief as a representing the stone table with four round projections (see Figure 98)—symbols of the four elements of the universe: earth, air, fire, water.

If you look at the map of this area from a great height, the mountain on which the dolmen was built clearly resembles a hooded human figure with outstretched arms and legs. Is it not similar to the tarot card? Is it the magician with the stone table (Figure 121)?

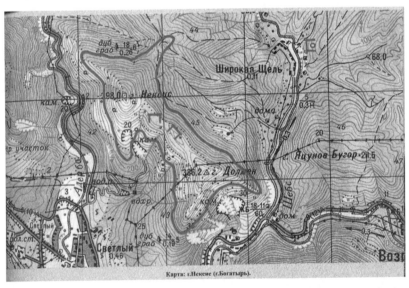

Figure 121. Human-like image of the Bogatyr (warrior) mountain with the images of dolmens.

Figure 122. Geometrical images on some of the dolmens. Water, heaven, and underworld fire (dolmen "Lunnyj," Gelendzhik area), left; water, mountains, and eternity symbols (dolmen "Chernomorka-1," Lazarevsky City, District of Sochi), center; eternity symbol in a circle framing the aperture (dolmen in Shirokaya Shchel, Gelendzhik area), right.

Symbols of the four elements are often represented on dolmens (Figure 122). Air is represented by the shape of the table (celestial sphere). Water is represented by horizontal wavy lines. Heaven and the underworld fire are depicted as lightning. Earth is symbolized by triangles resembling mountain ranges. In tarot cards, the "fifth element" is a horizontal "eight" above the magician's head (Figure 122), a symbol of eternity. On the dolmen it was represented by a circle framing the aperture in the center of the front plate.[4]

Because megaliths already existed

Figure 123. Image from the book *Malleus Maleficarum.*

when "modern" peoples discovered the structures, they started worshiping these constructions. They never knew who built the megaliths and believed they were built by gods or very ancient people: magicians and giants.

Christianity tried to reduce the power of the dolmens and associated them with devils. Thus, megaliths were depicted in the book *Mal-*

leus Maleficarum ("Molot Vedm" in Russian), a medieval treatise about witches, as a place of the devil (Figure 123).

However, because of their emanating power, megaliths, and dol-

mens in particular, were subconsciously associated with places of good power. This has been implemented in some architecture movements (see Part III, "Future of the Dolmens," for more information). Thus, architects placed figures of power, such as sculptures of angels and gods, on top and around dolmen-shaped architectural elements (Figure 124).

Figure 124. Sculptures of goddesses and angels on an oeil-de-boeuf architectural element.

Dolmens and Orbs

Dolmens are also famous for observing orbs (Figure 125). Many people believe that orbs are paranormal entities, such as ghosts or even aliens; skeptics maintain that these apparitions are completely explainable by photographic science.

Now you can decide for yourself if the orbs are something other than "a typically circular artifact on an

Figure 125. Orbs visible on a dolmen.

image, created as a result of flash photography illuminating a mote of dust or other particle."[5] You have enough evidence after reading all the above information about the dolmens. If you are interested in learning more about orbs, read Mya Gleny's *Orbs – The Gift of Light*.

Dolmen Healing and Spirituality

Hidden Power of the Dolmens

As this book has previously discussed, dolmens are made of stone with a high volume of quartz. Quartz (SiO_2) is a mineral with interesting characteristics. In particular, the piezoelectric ability to generate electric current under effects of mechanical deformation (compression or stretching) and to maintain a constant frequency oscillation (frequency stabilization). This characteristic is used in radio engineering. Under the influence of electricity, the quartz crystals generate ultrasound (a reverse piezoelectric effect). It was also established that under mechanical deformations, quartz is capable of generating radio waves.

R. Furdui argued that periodic compression and stretching of massive sandstone slabs, from which the dolmen was built, led to deformations of the myriad grains of quartz, which are part of the dolmen stone. Grains of quartz in sedimentary rock, including sandstone, are properly oriented for generating ultrasound due to the piezoelectric effect. That is why, apparently, megaliths, in order to obtain the necessary power for ultrasonic flow, required a minimum mass of stone, and is why one dolmen composed of five to six blocks together could weigh between 7 and 25 metric tons.[1]

The deformation of the dolmen's stone blocks was caused by the tidal action of the moon and the sun. Tidal waves due to the attraction of the moon lead to vertical movements, not only in ocean water but also in the layers of the earth's crust. Thus, at Moscow's latitude, the daily fluctuation of the earth's crust due to tidal influence is about 30 cm (11.8 in.). The height of the tidal wave in the earth's crust (as well as in the oceans) is constantly changing, depending on the location of the moon and sun in relation to the earth, revealing diurnal, monthly, and longer cycles. Is it because the builders of megaliths were interested in the movement of the moon that they needed to know the mode of operation of their "emitters" (see the "Dolmens and the Paleolithic Calendar" in Part I)?

The vertical elements of the dolmen (the walls) experienced the most deformation, especially in their lower parts. They underwent pressure not only from the most vertical slab but also from the roof of the dolmen. It is possible that "heel" stones placed under the walls of the dolmen, if there was no stone block at the bottom, could play a role in the acoustic system.

In the UK, scientists made an interesting discovery concerning Rollright, a megalithic monument on the border of Oxfordshire and Warwickshire. This structure consists of a circle of stones, a dolmen, and a menhir and is similar to other megalithic structures. Research started with a zoologist who investigated the flights of local bats in this region using an ultrasound receiver. He found that at certain times of the day the megalith emits ultrasounds, muffling the squeaking sound of bats. He informed scientists at Oxford about this "anomaly," which led to the "Dragon Project," an informal group of scientists under the lead of Dr. Don Robins that included physicists, radio engineers, chemists, and geologists. Robins described the project as follows:

Earth energy was the central point at issue. The protagonists of Earth energy suggested that it was a kind of synthesis of various forms of electromagnetic and mechanical energies, which arose from the earth's crust and interacted with solar and cosmic radiation. At certain times, on midsummer day for example, the energy became concentrated at certain points or nodes, or along lines between nodes, or so the theory went. Some protagonists went on to suggest that people with psychic powers or dowsers could detect those foci of energy, though ordinary mortals might be aware only of a vague 'atmosphere.' Some suggested that ancient, Neolithic people were receptive to the influence of those centres of energy and built their shrines and sepulchres upon them; and others suggested that our Stone Age and Bronze Age ancestors were even able to direct and augment that energy by linking the structures into a complex web, in a massive exercise in landscape engineering.[2]

Robins explained that, for example, menhir radiate ultrasound to a distance of 45 m (147.6 ft.) in diameter, as measurements have shown. Beyond this 45-meter zone, the ultrasound effect was not detected. Control measurements were made of nearby objects to Rollright—concrete structures and natural accumulations of sand blocks—but none of them radiated ultrasonic waves.

Oxford scientists hypothesized that the ultrasonic vibrations of this "Stone Age transmitter" were due to weak electrical currents, which in turn occur in the stones under the influence of solar radio waves. At the same time, they believed that the "energy of sound" of each individual stone is small in itself, but the exact location (geographical orientation) of all stones creates a total powerful energy flow.

A magnetic survey was also conducted, which revealed that the stone circle seems to shield the earth's magnetic field: inside the circle it was weakened. A spiral "belt" of an amplified magnetic field was also detected, making seven turns and going beyond the stone circle. It is suggested that this magnetic structure was created by the megalith's ancient builders by burrowing pieces of magnetite or other magnetic minerals within a circle (however this assumption has not been yet verified, since scientists did not conduct excavations inside the circle).

Interesting results were also obtained when measuring radioactivity at Rollright. The measurements showed short-term "bursts" of radioactivity, which increased threefold during the day and then decreased again. It is suggested that these fluctuations in radioactivity can be explained by changes in the level of groundwater containing radioactive components.

In 1988, Soviet scientist R. Furdui hypothesized that, based on the properties of megaliths, they (at least some of them) could be complex technical devices, namely generators of acoustic, and possibly electromagnetic, oscillations. He based his calculations on about 50 Caucasian dolmens for which V. Markovin, in his 1978 monograph, "Dolmens of the Western Caucasus," gives precise geometric parameters.

Furdui considered dolmens as large acoustic cavities and decided to find out which resonant frequencies they were tuned to. He treated them as Helmholtz resonators. Helmholtz resonance is a phenomenon in the resonance of air in a cavity, an example of which is the hum of an empty bottle from a stream of air directed perpendicular to its neck. The resonant frequency of the acoustic cavity depends on its maximum perimeter, which in the dolmen chamber is its perimeter at the bottom. Furdui constructed a graph-histogram of the perimeter chambers of Caucasian dolmens based on Markovin's data, obtaining an unexpected result.

It turned out that among more than two thousand dolmens there are only three types of predominate geometry. Most often (statistically most reliably) there are dolmens whose chamber perimeter is 720 cm (283.4 in.). In addition to this group, there are (statistically less reliable) larger buildings with a perimeter of 1,035 cm (407.5 in.) and a smaller size whose perimeter is 472 cm (185.8 in.). The resonant frequencies of such chambers are respectively equal to 23, 16, and 35 Hz. In other words, if energy were supplied to these dolmens (resonators) in some way, then they would make a sound precisely at such frequencies.

Furdui proposed that dolmens not only generated ultrasound but also radiated it in the form of a beam (searchlight effect), as evidenced by the structural features of dolmens. The dolmen chamber is a bell that widens from the back wall to the front. The typical dolmen had to generate a beam of ultrasonic vibrations, modulated by a sound frequency of 23 Hz, in the direction of the dolmen entrance.[3]

The geometry of the entrance played an important role, along with the angle of inclination of the dolmen walls. Usually the entrance hole is a form of a truncated cone, tapering from the front wall of the plate to the back, and thus representing a kind of a "shout." Perhaps the geometry of this speaker played a specific role in focusing the sound stream the dolmen generated.

Furdui theorized that since it was obviously difficult to determine the exact dimensions of the chamber, and since the physical (piezo-acoustic) properties of the stone from which the dolmens were made changed from place to place, a precise adjustment to the required sound frequency was required. For this purpose, the dolmen creators engraved drawings, which archaeologists call "ornaments," on the surface of the chamber walls (mainly the back wall) (Figure 126). Furdui is sure that these jagged lines, spirals, concentric circles, and other images played a role in the tuning circuits (attenuators) with which the required parameters of the dolmen sound were achieved.[4]

Figure 126. One of the so-called "ornaments" inside a dolmen at Mount Nexis.

Archaeologists call these ornaments "signs of water or mountains." However, Furdui analyzed them from a sound-generating point of view, and on one of the dolmens he found three types of zigzags in sizes (steps) of 5, 10, and 12.5 cm (roughly 2, 4, and 5 in.). Some of them are situated vertically, others horizontally. The steps of all three zigzag types are a multiple of the diameter of the hole of the dolmen, equal to 40 cm (15.7 in.). Apparently, during the exact adjustment of the dolmen, the "operator" regularly applied these zigzags to achieve the required sound frequency.[5]

How did the process of tuning the dolmen for the required sound frequency occur? Which standards were used? Furdui proposed the following technique. Dolmens that contain ancient burials also include ceramic pots with a specific ornamentation (Figure 127)—the so-called "grooved ware" with zigzag lines. These zigzag lines probably referred to the acoustic parameters to which the dolmen had to be adjusted or tuned. In this case, a pot with a zigzag-like ornament could be used as a receiver of sounds emitted by a dolmen. Applying zigzags to the dolmen's sounding walls, the priest achieved the maximum sound volume of the "singing" pot in resonance with the dolmen (similar to the Tibetan singing bowl that can resonate with musical instruments). The parameters of the zigzags were taken from the reference pattern on a pot. These standards were copied from much older samples, so this information was transmitted from generation to generation, even in the absence of written language.

Figure 127. Examples of pottery with grooved ornaments from the Bronze Age Catacomb culture in Caucasus.

However, in my personal opinion, these ceramics belong to a later culture that was not connected to the megalith builders. The reason is that pottery was not found in other similarly constructed megalithic structures. Of course, ancient pottery with grooved zigzag lines has been found in other parts of the world, such as England, Europe, and North and South America. This pottery, however, was not found inside local megaliths and no connection was made between them.

Work performed at Soviet scientific and medical institutions shows that focused ultrasound can indeed be used as an irritant. Its activating action in a number of cases is similar to natural stimulation and can cause tactile, taste, and a number of other sensations. It was discovered that the ultrasound effect occurs in the receptive neural structures located in the skin, muscles, bones, and joints of animals and humans.[6] Volunteers experienced an unpleasant sensation, which they compared to drilling on the skin.[7]

There is also information that low-frequency oscillations (13–25 Hz) leads to resonant oscillations of various human internal organs. Oscillations with a frequency of 25 Hz, after 30 minutes, caused an epileptic seizure. The effect of low-frequency oscillations that are close to the natural frequencies of internal organs, in particular the heart (6–12 Hz), can even be fatal.[8] The resonance frequencies of most of the Northern Caucasian dolmens were close to these values.

Thus, the geometrical parameters of the dolmen chambers indicate that these structures could generate low-frequency acoustic oscillations. It seems that these frequencies could be superimposed on the ultrasonic vibrations of dolmens, modulating them. But did the dolmens generate ultrasound and, if so, why? Indirect data indicate they indeed were able to do this. Most likely it was done through a piezoelectric effect. That is, when some natural crystals are squeezed or stretched, electrical charges appear on the edges of the crystals. This "hidden" power of the dolmens could have been used by ancient builders for various purposes. There are several theories for how this power could be applied.

Since the North Caucasian dolmens were built in areas along the zones of active geological faults (again, the question is how did ancient megalith builders choose these particular places?), one can assume another possible role of the dolmens. Some of them might have served as prediction devices for an imminent earthquake. It is known that before a strong earthquake, the tension in tectonic blocks grows significantly, producing foreshocks (minor tremors). All this can be detected by a sensitive acoustic device, such as a dolmen. If the dolmen began to "buzz," the priest-observer, who knows the dolmen properties, would sound the alarm, and the inhabitants of the neighboring villages would go into open spaces, drive cattle out of the barns, and take other preventive measures.

Maybe dolmens served as earthquake stabilizers? Dolmen vibrations could have been used in the same way as, for example, a giant pendulum was used in the Taipei 101 building in Taiwan. Such pendulums are known as a tuned mass dumper or harmonic absorber. They are used to reduce the mechanical vibrations of tall buildings and skyscrapers, especially during earthquakes.

Healing Power of the Dolmens

Another practical application of this powerful force could be for healing. We know, that ancient megaliths as well as dolmens were erected in places of power, that is, in zones of geomagnetic anomalies and, as a consequence, geopathogenic processes were observed. The Gaia theory views the planet as a single organism. Therefore, any place of power, on a planetary scale, can be considered as an acupuncture point of the given organism.

Russian scientist V. Vernadsky was among the first to perceive the earth as a single living organism in which different but closely related processes occur in the earth's three external spheres: lithosphere, hydrosphere, and atmosphere. Along with other scientists, Vernadsky developed the concept of another "sphere" that is part of all life on earth—the noosphere.[9] The noosphere is the sphere of human thought, and all spheres are connected and influence each other.

Just as acupuncture lines produce different health results in humans, influencing geomagnetic zones produces its own results, depending on the goal. Ancient peoples knew this and used megaliths as catalysts for affecting individual humans as well as group processes.

In Brittany, France, women especially would spend the night at a megalith to cure infertility or obtain blessings for a happy marriage. Similar customs existed among the inhabitants of ancient Wales and Scotland. On certain days of the year they lit bonfires at megaliths in sacrifice to the spirits of their ancestors.[10]

As discussed earlier, dolmens are built with sandstone or granite, which contain crystals. When dolmen blocks move due to the earth's vibrations, these crystals convert mechanical energy into electrical energy and vice versa. Therefore, dolmens generate high-frequency vibrations and electromagnetic waves.

Each dolmen was probably "tuned" to vibrate at a unique frequency to produce a specific effect on a person. A similar technique is used today, one variation of which is called the "Solfeggio frequencies." Solfeggio frequencies make up the ancient six-tone scale thought to have been used to balance energy and keep the body, mind, and spirit in harmony.[11] The six main Solfeggio frequencies are:

396 Hz: Liberating guilt and fear

417 Hz: Undoing situations and facilitating change

528 Hz: Transformation and miracles (DNA repair)

639 Hz: Connecting/relationships

741 Hz: Expression/solutions

852 Hz: Returning to spiritual order

American scientist Royal Raymond Rife made incredible progress in this field, offering "frequency therapy" that, according to him, treats a number of different conditions, including cancer. In the 1920s, he even created a machine, the Rife frequency generator, to use with his patients.[12]

Rife and his supporters believe that each disease or condition has its own electromagnetic frequency, and that finding that frequency and producing an impulse of the same frequency can kill or disable diseased cells. The Rife machine and other similar machines produce these low-energy waves.

Unfortunately, mainstream medicine does not embrace these ideas. The Rife machine has not been approved by the Food and Drug Administration (FDA) in America, and the American Cancer Society indicates that the FDA has warned companies that sell these machines not to make unproven claims.

The medical application of some megaliths is evidenced by a pattern on the back wall of one of the French dolmens in Gavrinis. This dolmen contains a strange relief in the form of a stylized human figure (Figure 128), consisting of parallel lines.[13] Some of these lines resemble human lines that are known to acupuncturists. However, most of the lines go far beyond the contours of the human body and instead resemble the lines of the human aura. Particularly distinguished on this relief are the heart and spine, energetically the most important organs.

Figure 128. Relief in the form of a stylized human figure in Gavrinis dolmen in France.

After a certain period of time, the functions of the dolmen can change (because of changes in the local biosphere, noosphere, etc.). Therefore, it is necessary to approach the study of megalithic structures with great care. Only people who are spiritually enlightened and well-intentioned may do this. The Adyghe people at the beginning of the 21st century claimed that anyone who goes to the "houses of eternity" without being called by the gods awaits a terrible punishment. However, anyone who sincerely wishes to use the mystical power of the dolmen can, if desired, join the mysteries of the universe and receive energy assistance as well as obtain answers to difficult questions.

The power of the dolmens can awaken talents and abilities that lay dormant in a person. It is possible to meet oneself, leading to unification with the earth, humanity, and the universe. This is the magic of true transfiguration. The only condition is an open heart and pure thoughts.

Each dolmen, like each human person, is different. Their vibrations, even if you are using a model or a photo, create and activate the energy field to help you find a way out of a difficult situation, understand the cause of a failure or disease, become wiser, or find your way to divine harmony.

According to V. Nikonov and D. Trost, a special ritual is required to feel the power of the dolmen energy. Select a time during the day when you have 20 to 30 minutes of free time. It is better in the morning, immediately after waking up, to set a tone for the whole day. Pick a time when it is possible to think, to understand what is happening, to dream about tomorrow. Look at a model or photos of dolmens, and choose one you feel "close" to that today. Determine the precise problem, goal, or most important question for you at that point that you want the dolmen help with. Determine what you want to change in yourself or in your life. Greet the spirit of the dolmen. Close your eyes and visualize the image of the selected dolmen, hold it in silence without being distracted by extraneous thoughts, and ask questions or ask the dolmen for help. Do this for about 15 to 20 minutes, asking questions and listening to the responses. Remember that one essential condition for communication with dolmens is purity of thought. When finished, thank the dolmen, and say good-bye to its spirit.[14]

Each dolmen has its own personality,[15] and people with extrasensory abilities can "map" each dolmen to specific psychic characteristics. For example, dolmens on the Kamyshovo (Reed) Hill are "healing dolmens." This group consists of seven dolmens that are located on the opposite bank of the Pshada River on the Kamyshovo Hill, about a 20-minute walk from the outskirts of Pshada.

Of course, it is always better to be in close vicinity to a specific dolmen when performing healing ceremonies or asking questions. However, to do this, you have to travel to North Caucasus. If you do not have this opportunity, you can use a replica of the dolmen or even a picture and perform the same ceremony you would do beside a "real" dolmen.

I have made a small clay replica of a dolmen for this specific purpose (Figure 129). When I need, I follow the ritual described above. I use this replica in various situations in life, even just to get into a better mood or to receive creative power. Believe me, it always works!

I think that's the real purpose of the dolmens—to heal, change you in positive ways, and help you live a healthy life.

Figure 129. Replica of a dolmen made by the author.

Dolmens and Living and Dead Waters

Some dolmens have human-made dents on their stone surface (Figure 130). The presence of the dents may indicate that the stone surface was once used as an altar.

Figure 130. Example of artificially made dents on the "moon" dolmen at Mount Nexis, near Gelendzhik.

Altars located on the western side of a dolmen, which represented the "dying" sun, were probably used at the equinoxes for offering sacrifices to the gods of death. On the other hand, altars on the eastern side, where the sun is "born," might have been used to collect the "healing" power of rainwater or dew. Here we can recall one of the motives of Slavic folklore. The water that was collected in the eastern stone dents may be associated with the water of life, and moisture accumulating in the western altar associated with the water of death. In Slavic folklore, "living water" has certain magical or supernatural properties. For example, in fairy tales, living water can revive a dead body. Conversely, dead water has the ability to heal wounds.

Part III

Future of the Dolmens

The secret of the dolmens and other remaining ancient megaliths may never be found, but nevertheless they have to be protected and preserved for future generations. Unfortunately, the local Russian government doesn't protect these ancient human monuments.

Lost Dolmens

Existing dolmens gradually disappear or fall into disrepair. The monuments are disassembled for construction blocks and defaced by vandals (Figure 131, 132, and 133).

Archaeologist and historian A. A. Formozov writes: For three or four decades, the Cossacks destroyed the ancient monuments, sometimes to get stone for roadway pavement, the foundations of dwellings, or even just for fun. Now in the Bogatyr road, only pieces of the broken plates stick out of the ground. The dolmens were destroyed before the archaeologists managed to seriously research them. Even where the roofs and walls have been preserved, everything has been dug up by treasure hunters, and the bones of buried and clay vessels are broken and thrown about. Therefore, our information about dolmens is very incomplete.[1]

Figure 131. Alley of dolmens on the Bogatyr road between the villages of Abadzekh and Novosvobodnaya (old name "Tsar").

Figure 132. The largest monolith dolmen on the Bogatyr road.

Figure 133. Destroyed dolmen. This dolmen stood on the bank of the Ade-goy River, near the village of Shapsugskaya. According to several eyewitness accounts on the side of this dolmen, there were some inscriptions.

The now-destroyed dolmen-monolith (Figure 134) in the village of Beregovoe (in the Gelendzhik district) was photographed by E. Felitsin[2] and described in detail by P. Uvarova in 1886. The dolmen was in the courtyard of a local resident, and in the front of the dolmen was carved a classical recess with an entrance hole. The photo shows that the dolmen was built from a large stone, the facade of which was made to imitate the side plates of the classic tiled dolmen The dolmen was carved entirely from a monolith of fine-grained sandstone, and inside was a square chamber with smoothly carved walls. The dolmen was 2.1 m (6.89 ft.) long, the back wall was 1.49 m (4.88 ft.) wide, the front wall was 1.6 m (5.25 ft.) wide, and the height was 1.4 m (4.59 ft.).[3]

The village of Beregovoe also had 10 other dolmens. Countess Praskovya Sergeevna Uvarova studied them and talked with local people about these stone structures built by ancient people. She suggested that, perhaps, they were culturally developed, and she emphasized the fact that these buildings needed to be guarded. This caused some

Figure 134. The destroyed dolmen-monolith in the village of Beregovoe.

displeasure among local religious figures, who did not recognize the "cultural" nature of pre-Christian people. After the countess left, the Cossacks destroyed all the dolmens, including this unique monolith (Figure 134). The remains were used for the foundation of the church in Beregovoe.[4]

A. Aseev, who wrote about megalithic structures, mourned:

> Protected by folk worship, megaliths of Brittany and the South Caucasus successfully survived up to this day. However dolmens were unlucky. In 1897, the founder of the museum of Ekaterinodar (former name of Krasnodar), E. D. Felitsyn lamented: "The Highlanders, our predecessors in the Trans-Kuban region, are all with great respect to the ancient monuments. Unfortunately, the Kuban Cossacks, having inherited their land, do not follow this laudable trait". Even before the revolution, hundreds of dolmens were destroyed. Often they were broken without a purpose, just to "experience the power"

Even intelligent engineers have contributed to the destruction of the monuments, using plates for crushed stone to build the Black Sea highway. Sadly, our tractor operators like to test their "power" on the dolmens to see "who will win"—will the tractor break the stone megalith or will the tractor break first. And here are the results: in 1885, the Bogatyr road had 360 dolmens, by 1928 only 20, and now there are none.

So dark and illiterate Adygeans did not damage the dolmens; people with a higher culture erased them from the face of the earth. The explanation for the paradox is that for the Adygeans, *syrpun* were sacred, and for the Russians, strange, unfamiliar and unnecessary."[5]

Preservation of Dolmens

Unfortunately, existing dolmens are not getting restored (Figures 135 and 136).

One of the reasons that it may not be possible to restore them to their previous grandeur is because local authorities do not really care how these ancient structures are restored (Figures 137 and 138). They are restoring them, but at what cost to these ancient structures?

Another reason may be that there is no government program to take on such tasks. Sometimes local officials try to repair some dolmens to attract tourism, and some private enthusiasts take the initiative to clean and protect the dolmens.

I think the preservation of the dolmens is an important task! These ancient monuments have to be preserved, not only for the study of these remarkable structures but for the sake of our ancestors. People in the future will also admire, as we do today, the ancient builders, their ingenuity, and their power of spirit.

Figure 135. Dolmen near the village of Kalezh in an old photo. (Photo from archive of Ekaterina Bogoslovskya)

Figure 136. Same dolmen in the village of Kalezh with a broken roof.

Figure 137. How a dolmen from the village of Shkhafit looked about a century ago. (Photo from archive of Ekaterina Bogoslovskya)

Figure 138. "Restored" dolmen from the above picture showing the dolmen submerged in concrete.

Appendix 1: Visiting the Dolmens

I f you decide to see the dolmens with your own eyes, your first stop will probably be Krasnodar, a vibrant city with a large international airport, and which is close to dolmen locations. If you visit Krasnodar, here is some helpful information from someone who was born there and knows the city well.

About Krasnodar

Krasnodar is located on the Kuban River about an hour from the Black Sea. The name Krasnodar could be translated as "the gift from the Red Army" (it was previously called Ekaterinodar, "the gift from the Empress Ekaterina," also known as Catherine the Great). Another possible translation is "the beautiful gift," based on the old Russian word "red" in the meaning of "beautiful." The latter version is my personal favorite, however, it is not clear from whom this gift was presented.

Krasnodar is the administrative center of Krasnodar Krai (region) and has a population of about one million. The region of Krasnodar is famous for "Krasnodar black tea," an excellent black tea, and the legendary Abrau-Durso champagne (my last name *Loza* in Russian means "grapevine"). During the existence of the Soviet Union, the Adygea Autonomous Area, with its capital at Maykop, also belonged to Krasnodar Krai. Now it is the Republic of Adygea within Krasnodar Krai.

It is safe and easy to travel to Krasnodar, which may not be as famous as other Russian cities. Krasnodar city is known for the Shukhov Tower (or the Shukhovskaya Tower), located in the center of the city (Figure 139), that used to be a water tower. It is now considered to be the city symbol, much like the Eiffel Tower in Paris.

International and Distinctive Cuisine

I have been always interested in the foods of other nationalities, and many international dishes are among my favorites. Many different nationalities live in Krasnodar—Russians, Ukrainians, Adyghe, Abkhaz, Armenians, Gruzinim (people of Georgia), Koreans, Tatars, and many others. When I lived there, the biggest bazaar was the central Sennoy Rynok ("straw market"). The many stalls there sold delicacies like Armenian *basturma* (pastrami) and *churchkhela* (candy), hot Georgian *khachapuri* (cheese-filled bread), "Korean" pickled carrots and eggplant, Ukrainian *salo* (salted pig's lard), Russian *pastila* (fruit candy), Tatar *chebureki* (deep-fried turnovers), *belyashi* (small beef pastries), and many other tasty and different foods.

At home, my grandmother made *forshmak* (chopped herring with apple and onions) and bouillon with *cklezcki* (chicken soup with plain dumplings), a traditional Jewish food. At my friends' homes, I was treated to traditional Russian food—*vareniki* (pierogi, dumplings with potatoes, cottage cheese, or cabbage filling) and *pelmeni* (small dumplings filled with mincemeat and onions).

Figure 139. Shukhov Tower is an example of one of the world's first hyperboloid structures and one of seven remaining towers by the engineer Shukhov.

In the former Soviet Union, there was little (if any) variety in sweets and chocolates. But kids are kids, and we always wanted to eat something sweet, or at least something different from our day-to-day school lunch. When I was in elementary school, we used to go to the local pharmacy and buy sweet glucose tablets and ascorbic acid powder in small paper bags. This powder is the vitamin C found in food that is used as a dietary supplement, and we liked its sour taste. Also, in the pharmacy, one could buy another unusual food that was popular among kids: hematogen. This was a nutrition bar whose main ingredients were black food albumin taken from processed cow's blood. Ascorbic acid powder and hematogen bars were sold to us without prescription and without questions from the pharmacist. As a chocolate substitute, we used to buy dry *kissel* (a viscous fruit dish popular as a dessert drink) in the food store. It was dry and didn't taste sweet but we ate these bars with much gusto. As kids, we also used to eat claver flowers (which we called "kashka") and acid produced by ants (formic acid). To get this ant acid "delicacy" we used a special process of inserting a hard plant stick (better than a weed stem) into the ants' nest and waited until they started attacking the stick. This left drops of their acid on it. Later we licked the stick and enjoyed the sour taste of the ant's acid.

Table 2. International foods available in Krasnodar

Chebureki		Dough stuffed with minced meat.
Belyashi		Dough pastry with meat filling.

Churchkhela		Armenian and Georgian national delicacy prepared from walnuts covered with grape juice mixed with flour.
Pastila		Russian sweet and sour delicacy made of whipped apple puree or sour apples.
Basturma		Armenian dried fillet of beef.
Khachapuri		Georgian cake with cheese. The name comes from the words "cheese" and "bread."
"Korean style" pickled carrots		My wife's recipe for making this pickled carrot is the best.
"Korean style" pickled eggplant		Eggplant stuffed with carrots, bell peppers, and other tasty things.
Salo		Cured slabs of fatback (rarely pork belly), with or without the skin. Available worldwide in Russian and Ukrainian food stores.

Other foods Krasnodar is known for are ones I grew up with. My grandmother used to get *ponchiki*, the best donuts I ever had, from the neighboring market. They were freshly baked and covered with white sugar powder. Other foods include *babka*, or macaroni and jam, and *korzh*, a poppy seed pastry soaked in milk.

At the time of Perestroika, Krasnodar's food stores were full of *nutria* meat (sometimes called "river rat"). Nutria (Figure 140) is known for its fur, which is very popular in Russia for winter hats, but Russian businessmen found that they could sell the meat

Figure 140. Nutria, Myocastor coypus.

to supermarkets. This meat, which tastes like rabbit, is very popular.

The international food was obviously not strange or bizarre from my point of view. Probably because of my love for this food, I've always been open to trying new foods, as long as people in another country ate it.

Appendix 2: Getting the Most from Your Trip

This chapter shares my experience of how to get more from visiting and exploring a new place. Whether you're traveling with a tourist group with a set itinerary and eat in "safe" restaurants with a tourist menu, or you're traveling on your own, these tips will be helpful. If planning your own trip, finding an English-speaking person could be a challenge, but if you want to learn more about a place, it's always more fun to talk to the locals and try the native foods.

Read as Much as You Can

In my opinion, you should do your homework before going on a trip; this will make it more enjoyable and interesting. I prefer to read as much as possible about the history, modern life, authentic cuisine, drinks, and customs of a country or territory before I visit. A good place to start is the Internet (for example Wikipedia, TripAdvisor, or a Google search). If you have time, it is always better to read a couple of books on the subject. (I use Amazon.com, and read the reviews first to help choose the right book.)

Make a List

After doing your research, you may feel ready to put together a list of places you want to visit and things you want to do, based on your personal interests. Estimate the amount of time you may need for any activity and start to put everything together in an itinerary. However, be open to discovering other places and activities once you're there that may alter you plans.

Pack Light

If you have to carry luggage by yourself, packing lightly is preferable. I always take two of everything (pants, shirts, underwear, shoes, etc.), plus one jacket and one sweater. While you wear the first set of clothes during the day, you've already washed the other set the evening before so that it will be dry and ready to wear when you return to your hotel room. In the evenings, wash the clothes you wore that day. I have only three types of shoes: sport sandals, walking shoes, and indoor plastic slippers (for a hotel shower or a swimming pool).

Do not forget to take your medications with you, as well as medicines for preventing diarrhea, treating blisters, or dealing with seasickness and colds, which may save your vacation.

Take your cellphone as well. It will serve as a modern Swiss Army Knife: flashlight, camera, translator, map (download the offline version first), communications device (phone calls, SMS, Skype, WhatsApp, etc.), information source (download information about the place you are visiting from the Internet and read as a guide when you're there), and many other things. A cellphone can also be used as a copier or a magnifying glass. Take a screenshot of a map route or a hotel booking confirmation, together with a map, so you won't need an Internet connection (sometimes one won't be available) when you have to find your hotel or show your booking confirmation at reception.

Do not forget to back up your photos, for example, to a cloud drive (use iCloud for iPhones or Google Drive for Android devices), as access to Google or its services may be blocked in some countries, such as China.

Also, it is a good idea to pack some toilet paper and wet napkins. In some countries (such as China) you may not find these "luxury items" when you most need them. Later, you may take a toilet paper roll (one you haven't finished) from a hotel room, but be ready for emergencies.

The goal is to have just one bag for all your things, with some room for souvenirs. I personally prefer a backpack on wheels.

Personal and Food Safety

"Better to be safe than sorry" is the motto of a successful trip. Here is some advice based on my personal experience.

Avoid drinking local tap water (including ice), brushing your teeth with tap water, and eating fresh fruits and vegetables, such as in salads. Even in large hotels, restaurants in some countries may not be "safe" with regard to this rule. Drink only bottled water (make sure the bottle was not previously opened—insist the wait person bring the bottle to your table unopened), or boil the water in your hotel.

Once I was sick in India after eating bean sprouts in a very respectful hotel restaurant and again in Mexico after brushing my teeth. Being sick can spoil your travels for several days. If you do get sick, clean your stomach by drinking plenty of water (bottled or boiled water). Try to vomit after drinking a large amount of water and disinfect your stomach by eating things such as turmeric powder.

Avoid wandering after dark in nontourist places and empty streets. Before booking a hotel, find out if it is located in a safe district.

Withdraw money at a bank rather than at a street ATM. Do not take a large wad of money out of your pocket—a good idea is to put a small amount in one pocket and the rest in another. Pay at the store or for a taxi from the pocket where you have the small amount of money.

Most of the above tips apply to countries with relatively high poverty and crime rates. The majority of people are welcoming to tourists, but I recommend being vigilant in any foreign country, especially if you don't speak the local language, don't know the local customs, or don't follow the local news about the political situation. Remember, it's better to be safe than sorry!

Lost in Translation

Sometimes it may be difficult to communicate with a taxi driver or a restaurant waiter if a country you are visiting is not particularly English-speaking. These days, you can download a cellphone app, such as Google Translate, that does audio and visual translations. This kind of app can be very useful; I have found that phrase books are not as useful as a translation app. Test the app in offline mode to make sure you have downloaded all the necessary dictionaries for offline usage. Of course, you may have both, but finding the right sentence in a phrase book and correctly pronouncing it may be a challenge.

Personnel at large hotels may speak some English, as well as people at the airports and rail stations. Subway stations may have English translations for station names; car announcements also may be in English.

In museums, check for audio guides in English, as some museums do not provide English descriptions with their artifacts, but may have English audio guides with information. If you want more information when visiting a new place, hire an English-speaking guide. Be careful, however, as sometimes these guides may not really be knowledgeable about the place or may not speak understandable English. Check their language knowledge by chatting with them for a while.

Ask someone who speaks English to write the name of the place you want to visit in the local language. This will help when asking a taxi driver to take you somewhere. Always take the business card of the hotel you're staying at with you, as this can be useful in finding your way back to the hotel.

Also check the Internet for English-teaching groups in your country of destination. They will be happy to meet you at the airport and show you around for free.

Transportation Tips

If you travel by yourself, make sure you have a good map. Do not rely on buying a map at your destination, as you may not find one, or you may not find one in English. Usually, your hotel will have free maps of the area, including popular sightseeing spots. If not, go to any other hotel (preferably a large one) and ask for a free map.

When my wife and I go someplace in the city, we prefer to take a bus instead of a subway. Riding a bus may be a cheaper option as well as giving you a free sightseeing tour, while you won't see the city riding underground in a subway. Take a seat by the window and enjoy the ride!

Another option is to take a taxi, but be ready for a couple of tricks taxi drivers may use. Always make sure that the taximeter is on and is set to the initial fare. Once, when traveling in Vietnam, our taxi driver set the meter so that it added the fare very quickly. We immediately asked him to stop, but he pretended not to understand the command "Stop" and traveled for a couple of blocks more. For those five minutes, we paid taxi fare equal to an hour's trip. If we hadn't noticed the speed of the meter, we could have been victims of this large scam.

If a taxi doesn't have a meter, agree on a price before the ride. If you agree with a driver on a flat fare, be ready should they try to increase the fare while driving. Sometimes they may use lame excuses such as "mucho traffico" or "I haven't calculated properly the amount of time it would take for us to go there" or something else. Be firm, and don't agree to pay more than you initially agreed to. Usually when they see that you are not going to pay more, they will gladly accept the initial payment.

Another option is to hire a private driver. Ask the concierge at your hotel to recommend one, and make sure the driver speaks a fair amount of English (literally, test their English). Agree on a firm amount for the whole trip at the beginning. As with other taxi drivers, do not agree to any payment increases if the driver comes up with excuses once you are already far from the city. You can always find another driver who can continue the trip.

A good practice is to take your driver out for a meal with you. This will give you an opportunity (with the help of your driver) to go to a good restaurant that only local people may know about, try local food, and communicate with a waiter.

Choosing a Place to Eat

Another dilemma when traveling is where to eat. On the one hand, you want to try authentic local food, and on the other, you have to make sure that you don't "waste your appetite" on some "tourist food" that claimed to be local or, worse, become sick from the food. And do not waste your appetite on some random place that catches your eye when you feel hungry. One commonsense observation to consider: real, authentic local food does not have to be expensive. Local people do not go to upscale restaurants on a daily basis.

Of course, you could also go to a local supermarket or food store for local food—I pay particular attention to the fruit and vegetable sections as well as the meat and fish departments. You can always find something "country-specific," seasonal, or even unique. Take the food to your hotel and enjoy the "room service." It is also a good practice to find a hotel or apartment with a kitchenette. This way you're not limited to buying precooked food but can try something from the raw food section.

If you want to know more about a country, you have to go to the local market. There you will see strange and unusual foods as well as meet local people (who may be traditionally dressed) that you may not meet on the streets. My favorite is the fish market. The variety of sea products, especially in countries with access to the ocean, is enormous. Visiting a fish market could be as exciting and informative as visiting an aquarium and nature museum at the same time.

You can buy foods you want to try from the stalls and ask any small restaurant in the market to cook them for you. Be adventurous and don't be shy—try some new and unusual food—the locals will be happy to cook it for you in the traditional way.

Another option is to try street food. To be on the safe side, as well as to find good food, follow some commonsense rules. Always look for a vendor who has a line—do not buy from a vendor who has no other customers. Buy just-cooked hot food; do not buy ready-to-eat food that was displayed at a stall for who knows how long.

You could also rent room and board from a local family. However, in this case, you will be limited to whatever food is cooked for you. It is always better to explore local cuisine by yourself.

In my experience, asking the hotel to recommend a good place to eat may not always bring you to a good restaurant. People's tastes are different, and in many cases you may be referred to an expensive place that the person referring has never visited. The person may be getting a small commission from the restaurant owner for bringing new clients, or the person may recommend a place that they think tourists have to go to.

Based on my experience, the following are some well-tried practices for choosing a restaurant with authentic local cuisine. Look for a place based on the following criteria:

- The restaurant seems to have many local customers and no tourists. This is always a sign of good and inexpensive food.
- The menus are not in English.
- No replica food items are on display to attract tourists for easy dish ordering.

If the restaurant has no English-speaking personnel to help you with your order, look around to see what other people are eating. You can always point to a dish on another table that you want to try. Ask for the name of the dish and write it down, or ask your water to do this for you in the native language. This will help you to order it next time (assuming you like it).

Remember that the food is as fresh as your proximity to the food source. Do not order seafood if the city is not on the sea. Try other foods the place is famous for and whose ingredients are locally sourced.

Check out the restaurant's toilet first. It doesn't have to be modern, but it has to be clean. That reflects on their sanitation policy. If they care about their washrooms, it is a reflection of their kitchen policy as well, although sometimes we don't have a choice, do we?

One more tip. If the restaurant has a Michelin star and you don't want to spend a fortune for your meal, go there for lunch. The portions may be smaller but your meal will be cheaper and the food is the same quality as dinner.

Check Visa Requirements

Always check visa entry requirements. Sometimes, you may be unable to obtain a visa when you arrive at a country. Some countries, like Tibet, which is considered Chinese territory, require a special advance permit, even if you already have a Chinese visa. Some countries require a "Letter of Invitation" (for example, Turkmenistan) before you can apply for a visa, and you may need to obtain such a letter far in advance. Contact the country's travel bureau for help with getting this letter.

Also, make sure to book your hotel in advance, as some countries may deny you a visa based on the fact that you don't know where you'll be staying. This happened to me a couple of times, for example, when visiting Turks and Caicos Islands.

Make sure to have copies (preferably in color) of the first and visa pages of your passport. It is a good idea to keep a copy of your passport pages in your luggage in case it gets lost so that when it's opened, they'll have information for getting your luggage back to you.

Prepare Sightseeing in Advance

Before visiting another country, make a list of places you want to visit or special events you want to participate in. Sometimes, you may have to book a visit to a specific place as much as several months in advance.

For example, places like the Alhambra in Spain, the Hypogeum in Malta, the London Tower Ceremony of the Keys in Britain, or the Burj Khalifa, Dubai's tallest building, require booking in advance, preferably several months before.

Plan your trip accordingly. If you have an opportunity, plan your visit in conjunction with a festival or special event in the country. In this case, book a hotel several months in advance, as it may be impossible to find a hotel at the time of the event. Check the hotel's cancellation policy, and make sure you can cancel the booking in advance if it turns out you won't be able to make the trip.

Respect Local Customs and Traditions

You may be surprised, but some countries have laws that are completely different from the laws where you live. Even if you consider some laws senseless or ridiculous, disobeying them may get you into trouble. For example, make sure to disable the GPS coordinates recorded in your digital camera when visiting China, and do not take pictures of children when visiting some Asian countries. Actually, it is good practice to always ask for permission before taking pictures of local people, inside stores, or filming events. In Singapore, you may even be fined up to $1,000 as a first-time offender chewing gum!

Search the Internet in advance for such unusual laws and do not forget to follow them while you are visiting.

Money and Other Necessities

It's a good idea to have a small amount of local money with you when you arrive in a new country to pay for such things as the taxi to the hotel. You can purchase more money when you're there, but be ready when you arrive, as an exchange place may be closed, or not even exist, along with bank machines. The safest way to get more cash is to buy money in a bank or at your hotel.

Keep money in a safe place, preferably somewhere in your inner pockets. Have only small bills accessible in your pockets and do not flash money in public places or when buying something.

Take two or three different credit cards with you (such as a Master-Card and a Visa). Keep a printed copy of your credit cards with a bank phone number (do not copy the back side with the CVV number) with you in case you have to report them stolen. It is a good idea to alert your credit card companies in advance where and when you'll be traveling. If you don't, when you go to charge something (or check in at your hotel), they may think your card is stolen and shut down your account. Some credit card companies may send a text alert or e-mail, but if you don't have Internet access, you may not receive these.

A couple more things worth mentioning. If you rent a car, check your credit card after filling the gas tank and paying with your credit card. Gas stations are common places for credit card fraud.

One rule that my wife and I have learned the hard way regards buying good souvenirs. When you a see a suitable souvenir, buy it on the spot. Do not rely on buying it down the road. You may never find the same one. We have a saying, "When you see it, grab it!" The same applies to the toilet: when you see one, use it. You may not find another one for some time.

Sometimes it is a good idea to go to another terminal at the airport to buy souvenirs. The domestic terminals may have different souvenirs, and most of the time they are much cheaper than at the international terminal. Do not forget to bargain, even in the "big" stores!

Miscellaneous Tips

Today, with the number of travel websites available, you no longer need a travel agent to book a trip. Travel agents charge commissions for doing pretty much the same job that you could do yourself.

Keep a journal of your trip. You may later forget the names of the places you visited or food you liked. Reading a travel log from several years ago can refresh your memories and remind you of the good time you had.

It's always beneficial to learn several words in the country's native language. Words like *hello, yes, thanks,* and especially *no* can always come in handy.

Do not rely on reviews of sightseeing trips or hotels. You may have a different experience or tastes, and sometimes business owners write five-star reviews. I usually go straight to the three-star reviews for objective opinions, skipping the five- and one-star reviews as possible biased.

Do not use "free" public Wi-Fi networks to check your bank accounts online. At the least, do this at your hotel using the "official" hotel network. You can also use Google's Wi-Fi Assistant on Android devices to connect securely to open public Wi-Fi networks. Whenever you connect to an open Wi-Fi hotspot using Wi-Fi Assistant, the connection is protected by an encrypted virtual private network operated by Google. Check your Android device for how to enable the Wi-Fi Assistant.

If you are interested in more good tips for safe and enjoyable trips, an excellent source, although out of print, is Alison Tilley's *Travel Tips* book.[1]

Conclusion

I encourage you to travel to places described in this book. See everything with your own eyes. Try food that you've never eaten before. Do not rely on anyone's opinion. As the song "Beached" (from the move *The Beach*) says, "Never resist the unfamiliar. Never fail to be polite. And never outstay your welcome. Just keep your mind open and suck in the experience."

And as the Russian proverb goes, "Better to see something once than to hear about it a hundred times!" Life is short—enjoy it!

Image Credits

Figure 1. Walker, E. (2018). *North Caucasus maps*. [online] Eurasian Geopolitics. Available at: https://eurasiangeopolitics.com/north-caucasus-maps/ [Accessed 2 Sep. 2018].

Figure 2. Markovin, V. *Dol'meny Zapadnogo Kavkaza* [Dolmens of the Western Caucasus]. (Moscow: Nauka, 1978). p. 95. (*left*). Мария Анашина. Путешествия с Марией Анашиной. (2018). Поездка в Геленджик - отдых пляжный и не только. [online] Available at: https://anashina.com/poezdka-v-gelendzhik/ [Accessed 27 Sep. 2018].

Figure 3. PastVu. (2018). *1900—1917 Дольмен*. [online] Available at: https://pastvu.com/p/185153 [Accessed 2 Sep. 2018].

Figure 4. Puteshestviaporossii.ru. (2018). *Дольмены Геленджика*. [online] Available at: http://puteshestviaporossii.ru/dolmeny-gelendzhika/ [Accessed 2 Sep. 2018].

Figure 5. Helperia. (2016). *Кавказские дольмены - Helperia*. [online] Available at: https://helperia.ru/a/kavkazskije-dolymeny [Accessed 2 Sep. 2018].

Figure 6. Ilia-romantic.narod.ru. (2009). *Дольмены у рек Пшада и Жане 2009*. [online] Available at: http://ilia-romantic.narod.ru/krd2009/dolmeny_2009.html [Accessed 5 Sep. 2018].

Figure 7. Abornev, I. (2016). *Поход выходного дня - дольмены Виноградного ущелья. 18.02.2016*. [online] Privetsochi.ru. Available at: http://privetsochi.ru/blog/walking/61933.html [Accessed 5 Sep. 2018].

Figure 8. Megalithica.ru. (2017). *Дольмен Калежтам 2 — урочище Джеожтам - MEGALITHICA.RU*. [online] Available at: https://megalithica.ru/dolmen-kalezhtam-2-urochishhe-dzheozhtam.html [Accessed 5 Sep. 2018].

Figure 9. Экскурсия дня). (2015). *Экскурсия по Геленджикскому району (4 дня)*. [online] Dolmenkavkaz.ru. Available at: http://dolmenkavkaz.ru/raspisanie-2015/ekskursiya-po-dolmens-of-gelendjik/ [Accessed 5 Sep. 2018]. *(left)*; Чёрт побери. (2017). *Научная версия назначения дольменов. Доказано технически (5 фото). Чёрт побери.* [online] Available at: http://chert-poberi.ru/interestnoe/nauchnaya-versiya-naznacheniya-dolmenov-dokazano-tehnicheski-5-foto-2.html [Accessed 5 Sep. 2018]. *(right)*

Figure 10. Xn-----elcz3ar7b6c.xn--p1ai. (2018). *33 водопада+Волконский дольмен - Экскурсии в Сочи.* [online] Available at: http://xn-----elcz3ar7b6c.xn--p1ai/ekskursii-v-sochi/33-vodopada-volkonskiy-dolmen [Accessed 5 Sep. 2018]. *(left)*; Markovin, V. *Dol'meny Zapadnogo Kavkaza* [Dolmens of the Western Caucasus]. (Moscow: Nauka, 1978). p. 181 *(right)*.

Figure 11. Loza, B.

Figure 12. Отдыхающим на заметку, Дольмены района, Отель в Лермонтово. (2018). *Дольмены Туапсинского района - где находятся, как добраться до дольменов Туапсе.* [online] Xn--b1aahb2abiicgbbuwj6m.xn--p1ai. Available at: http://xn--b1aahb2abiicgbbuwj6m.xn--p1ai/zametki/dolmeny-tuapsinskogo-rayona/ [Accessed 5 Sep. 2014]. *(left)*; Dolmen-kavkaz.ucoz.ru. (2018). *Интересные дольмены Адыгеи - Форум.* [online] Available at: http://dolmen-kavkaz.ucoz.ru/forum/13-165-1 [Accessed 5 Sep. 2018]. *(right)*.

Figure 13. Megalithica.ru. (2017). Дольмен Пригородный 2 - MEGALITH-ICA.RU. [online] Available at: https://megalithica.ru/dolmen-prigorod-nyi-2.html [Accessed 24 Sep. 2018]. (left). Terra-xx.narod.ru. (2018). *Мир мегалитов - Фотографии дольменов.* [online] Available at: http://terra-xx.narod.ru/f1.htm [Accessed 5 Sep. 2018]. (right).

Figure 14. Privetsochi.ru. (2018). *Дольмены - ретроспектива.* [online] Available at: http://www.privetsochi.ru/blog/history/52970.html [Accessed 5 Sep. 2018]. *(left)*; Matjashov, S. (2011). *Поиски дольменов в районе аула Псебе.* [online] Stasmat.livejournal.com. Available at: https://stasmat.livejournal.com/11537.html [Accessed 5 Sep. 2018]. *(right)*.

Figure 15. Олег Ложечников. Life-trip.ru. (2018). *Блог Олега Лажечникова Life-trip.ru.* [online] Available at: http://life-trip.ru [Accessed 5 Sep. 2018]. *(left)*; Privetsochi.ru. (2018). *Дольмены - ретроспектива.* [online] Available at: http://www.privetsochi.ru/blog/history/52970.html [Accessed 5 Sep. 2018].*(right)*.

Figure 16. Xn----8sbaaijhuxcfmok3rma.xn--p1ai. (2018). Дольмены Северного Кавказа. Река Жане.. [online] Available at: http://xn----8sbaaijhuxcfmok3rma.xn--p1ai/jhane.htm [Accessed 24 Sep. 2018]. *(left)*; Anon, (2018). [online] Available at: http://votezde.org/d-12482-dol-

men-solnechnuy.html [Accessed 24 Sep. 2018].*(right)*.
Figure 17. New.cosmoenergy.ru. (2018). *Дольмены в поселке Джубга. Фонд духовной культуры.* [online] Available at: http://new.cosmoenergy.ru/photogallery/dolmeny_djubga.html [Accessed 9 Sep. 2018]. *(left)*.
Filevskayalinia.livejournal.com. (2011). *Дольмены Жане (недалеко от Геленджика).* [online] Available at: https://filevskayalinia.livejournal.com/34160.html [Accessed 9 Sep. 2018]. *(right)*.
Figure 18. Histoforum.net. (2008). Johan Picardt. [online] Available at: http://histoforum.net/hunebeddenbo/picardt.htm [Accessed 9 Sep. 2018].
Figure 19. Cpa-bastille91.com. (2012). Dolmen de Bagneux – Saumur – Le Dolmen vu du côté Sud | Cartes Postales Anciennes. [online] Available at: http://www.cpa-bastille91.com/dolmen-de-bagneux-saumur-le-dolmen-vu-du-cote-sud/ [Accessed 9 Sep. 2018]. *(left)*. Dolmenes.blogspot.ca. (2012). *Dolmenes y megalitos del mundo.* [online] Available at: http://dolmenes.blogspot.ca/ [Accessed 9 Sep. 2018]. *(right)*.
Figure 20. Softelectro.ru. (2014). Dolmen. [online] Available at: http://softelectro.ru/dolmen_his.html [Accessed 24 Sep. 2018].
Figure 21. Softelectro.ru. (2014). [online] Available at: http://www.softelectro.ru/dolmen_118.pdf [Accessed 9 Sep. 2018].
Figure 22. Privetsochi.ru. (2015). *Дольмены - ретроспектива.* [online] Available at: http://www.privetsochi.ru/blog/history/52970.html [Accessed 9 Sep. 2018]. *(left)*. New.cosmoenergy.ru. (2018). *Дольмены на реке Жане. Фонд духовной культуры..* [online] Available at: http://new.cosmoenergy.ru/photogallery/dolmeny_jane.html [Accessed 16 Sep. 2018]. *(center)*. La-viento.livejournal.com. (2006). Возрождение. [online] Available at: https://la-viento.livejournal.com/58083.html [Accessed 9 Sep. 2018]. *(right)*.
Figure 23. Vladimir Yashkardin. "Dolmens. Pamjati Vladimira Ivanovicha Markovina [In memory of Vladimir Ivanovich Markovin]". 2014. http://www.softelectro.ru/dolmen.html [Accessed 9 Sep. 2018].
Table 1. Леонтьев, К. (2014). Геленджик октябрь 2014. Путешествия и личные фото. [online] Kleontev.ru. Available at: http://kleontev.ru/travel-and-photos/gelendzhik-oktjabr-2014/ [Accessed 24 Sep. 2018]. The Megalithic Portal. (2005). Le Grand Dolmen de Bagneux. [online] Available at: http://www.megalithic.co.uk/article.php?sid=6333738 [Accessed 9 Sep. 2018]. Колтыпин, А. (2018). Дольмены Кавказа. Конструкции дольменов (окрестности г.Геленджик, Россия). Часть 3. Конструкции дольменов - Земля до потопа: исчезнувшие континенты и цивилизации. [online] Dopotopa.com. Available at: http://www.dopotopa.com/konstruktsii_dolmenov_gelendzhik_rossia.html [Accessed 24 Sep. 2018]. Megalithica.ru. (2012). Dolmen-kavkaz.ucoz.ru. (2010). технологиче-

ские особености дольменов. - Страница 4 - Форум. [online] Available at: http://dolmen-kavkaz.ucoz.ru/forum/4-5-4 [Accessed 25 Sep. 2018]. Stuart, A. (2018). Easter Island. [online] Stuartgreenphotos.com. Available at: http://stuartgreenphotos.com/?page_id=8661 [Accessed 25 Sep. 2018]. Dolmen-kavkaz.ucoz.ru. (2010). технологические особености дольменов. - Страница 5 - Форум. [online] Available at: http://dolmen-kavkaz.ucoz.ru/forum/4-5-5 [Accessed 25 Sep. 2018]. Lesogorye.com. (2018). Новости — Гостиница "Лесогорье". [online] Available at: http://lesogorye.com/news/ [Accessed 25 Sep. 2018]. maestroviejo. (2018). SIMBOLOS PREHISTÓRICOS Y ASTRONOMÍA DE NEWGRANGE. [online] Available at: http://selenitaconsciente.com/?p=186710 [Accessed 25 Sep. 2018]. Новости Солнечной Системы. (2018). Загадочные мегалитические комплексы Республики Адыгея. [online] Available at: https://helionews.ru/71777-zagadochnye-megaliticheskie-kompleksy-respubliki-adygeya.html [Accessed 25 Sep. 2018]. Anon, (2007). [online] Available at: http://lah-ru.1gb.ru/expedition/peru2007-2/08ollaytaitambo.htm [Accessed 25 Sep. 2018]. Avtoturistu.ru. (2016). Не нужен нам берег турецкий ... Продолжение. / Путешествия НЕ на автомобилях! / Автотуристу.РУ - автопутешествия и автотуризм: отчёты, трассы и дороги, в Европу на машине, прокладка маршрута!. [online] Available at: https://avtoturistu.ru/blog/travel/%D0%BD%D0%B5_%D0%B-D%D1%83%D0%B6%D0%B5%D0%BD_%D0%BD%D0%B0%D0%BC_%D0%B1%D0%B5%D1%80%D0%B5%D0%B3_%D1%82%D1%83%D1%80%D0%B5%D1%86%D0%BA%D0%B8%D0%B9_%D0%B-F%D1%80%D0%BE%D0%B4%D0%BE%D0%BB%D0%B6%D0%B5%D0%BD%D0%B8%D0%B5.story [Accessed 25 Sep. 2018]. Insiderrevelations.ru. (2014). Анализ следов Древних Цивилизаций (ДЦ) земли.. [online] Available at: http://www.insiderrevelations.ru/forum/forum3/topic2812/?PAGEN_1=16 [Accessed 25 Sep. 2018]. Bushido.ru. (2012). Bushido.ru - Бусидо - Путь воина - Портал боевых искусств. Геленджик. Дольмены. Море, воздух и земля.. [online] Available at: http://www.bushido.ru/interaktiv/blogi/colred/gelendzhik_dol_meny_more_vozduh_i_zemlya/?p=4 [Accessed 25 Sep. 2018]. KakZachem.ru. (2018). 10 самых старых зданий в мире. [online] Available at: http://kakzachem.ru/10-samyh-staryh-zdanij-v-mire/ [Accessed 25 Sep. 2018]. Sharikov, U. and Komissar, O. *Dol'meny Kavkaza. Geologicheskie aspekty I tehnologii stroitel'stva [Dolmens of the Caucasus. Geological Aspects and Technologies of construction].* (Krasnodar, 2011). p. 169. Белых, В. (2017). Дальмены.. [online] Rodovoj.blogspot.com. Available at: http://rodovoj.blogspot.com/2017/03/blog-post_14.html?m=1 [Accessed 25 Sep. 2018]. Markovin, V. Dol'meny Zapadnogo Kavkaza [Dolmens of the Western

Caucasus]. (Moscow: Nauka, 1978). p. 132. Monsangelorum.net. (2017). Theory of Mind, Polygonal Masonry, Ancient Sea Kings, Metal Coupling Keys | mons angelorum. [online] Available at: http://www.monsangelorum.net/?p=28857 [Accessed 25 Sep. 2018]. Humanpast.net. (2018). Building in South America. [online] Available at: http://humanpast.net/shelter/separated/samericashelter.htm [Accessed 25 Sep. 2018].

Figure 24. Loza, B.

Figure 25. Showbell.ru. (2002). Встреча с дольменами. [online] Available at: http://www.showbell.ru/goroda/?st=gelendzhik2 [Accessed 9 Sep. 2018] and Loza, B.

Figure 26. Ordenxc.org. (2003).» Карачаево-Черкесская республика. Лесо-Кяфарь (Шпиль) ||| Орден Хранителей Смерти. [online] Available at: http://ordenxc.org/library/myortvye-goroda/karachaevo-cherkesskaya-respublika-leso-kyafar-shpil/ [Accessed 9 Sep. 2018].

Figure 27. Oilismastery.blogspot.com. (2009). Atlantis Art of Nicholas Roerich. [online] Available at: http://oilismastery.blogspot.com/2009/09/atlantis-art-of-nicholas-roerich.html [Accessed 9 Sep. 2018].

Figure 28. Коношонкин, Д. (2017). Шумерский город Ур: что произошло за последние 90 лет. [online] Энгурра. Available at: http://engur.ru/7818 [Accessed 17 Sep. 2018].

Figure 29. Newsmir.info. (2016). В Кабардино-Балкарии найдено захоронение людей с длинными черепами. [online] Available at: http://newsmir.info/590074 [Accessed 17 Sep. 2018].

Figure 30. Loza, B.

Figure 31. Metro.co.uk. (2008). *Tree man returns, looks less like a tree | Metro News*. [online] Available at: https://metro.co.uk/2008/08/27/tree-man-returns-looks-less-like-a-tree-432265 [Accessed 9 Sep. 2018].

Figure 32. Xissufotoday.space. (2016). Дольмены Западного Кавказа Western Caucasus Dolmens – Space track. [online] Available at: https://xissufotoday.space/2016/01/western-caucasus-dolmens-2 [Accessed 9 Sep. 2018]. *(left)*. Xn--80aaglbiyc0ahcmfq.xn--p1ai. (2018). Дольмен в поселке Каткова Щель. [online] Available at: http://xn--80aaglbiyc0ahcmfq.xn--p1ai/dolmen-v-poselke-katkova-shchel/ [Accessed 17 Sep. 2018]. *(right)*.

Figure 33. Mullen, R. (2017). Back to Palenque and The Temple of the Inscriptions. [online] Robintalkscookstravels.blogspot.com. Available at: http://robintalkscookstravels.blogspot.com/2017/03/my-second-visit-to-palenque-and-temple.html [Accessed 9 Sep. 2018].

Figure 34. Loza, B.

Figure 35. Spagyria.ru. (2018). Дольмены Северного Кавказа. Назначение дольменов – авторская версия.... [online] Available at: http://www.spagyria.ru/dolmen2.htm [Accessed 25 Sep. 2018]. Saphronov.msk.ru, (2018).

[online] Available at: http://saphronov.msk.ru/sajeni/dolmens/index.html [Accessed 9 Sep. 2018].

Figure 36. En.wikipedia.org. (2018). Sanchi. [online] Available at: https://en.wikipedia.org/wiki/Sanchi#Stupa_1_Western_Gateway [Accessed 9 Sep. 2018]. En.wikipedia.org. (2017). Loza, B.

Figure 37. Trocadero. (2018). Hokora Stone Hut Shinto Buddha Jizo Edo 18th c. (item #574763). [online] Available at: https://www.trocadero.com/stores/ganymede/items/574763/Hokora-Stone-Hut-Shinto-Buddha-Jizo-Edo-18th [Accessed 9 Sep. 2018]. (left). Trocadero. (2018). Stone Hokora God-House Shinto Edo 18 c. (item #729516). [online] Available at: https://www.trocadero.com/stores/ganymede/items/729516/Stone-Hokora-God-House-Shinto-Edo-18 [Accessed 9 Sep. 2018].(right).

Figure 38. Megalithica.ru. (2017). Дольмен урочища Клады 3 - MEGA-LITHICA.RU. [online] Available at: https://megalithica.ru/dolmen-urochishha-kladyi-1.html [Accessed 9 Sep. 2018].

Figure 39. Loza, B.

Figure 40. Commons.wikimedia.org. (2018). File:Schloss Chenonceau Ochsenauge.jpg - Wikimedia Commons. [online] Available at: https://commons.wikimedia.org/wiki/File:Schloss_Chenonceau_Ochsenauge.jpg [Accessed 25 Sep. 2018].. Ingalls, J. (2017). Dragon-proofing: why skyscrapers in Hong Kong have holes. [online] Archinect. Available at: https://archinect.com/news/article/150000479/dragon-proofing-why-skyscrapers-in-hong-kong-have-holes [Accessed 25 Sep. 2018].

Figure 41. Ancientresource.com. (2017). Ancient Resource: Authentic Ancient Hittite Artifacts For Sale. [online] Available at: http://www.ancientresource.com/lots/hittite.html [Accessed 9 Sep. 2018].

Figure 42. En.wikipedia.org. (2018). Lingodbhava. [online] Available at: https://en.wikipedia.org/wiki/Lingodbhava [Accessed 9 Sep. 2018]. En.wikipedia.org. (2017). Yoni. [online] Available at: https://en.wikipedia.org/wiki/Yoni [Accessed 9 Sep. 2018].

Figure 43. Bluffton.edu. (2002). La Venta Park, Tabasco, Mexico. [online] Available at: https://www.bluffton.edu/homepages/facstaff/sullivanm/mexico/olmec/olmec2.html [Accessed 9 Sep. 2018].

Figure 44. HISTORIA, CIENCIA, AZTECAS, MITO, CALENDARIO, ANTROPOLOGÍA. (2013). OLMECAS, SERPIENTES Y AGUA. LA VENTA, TABASCO, MÉXICO. [online] Available at: https://2012profeciasmayasfindelmundo.wordpress.com/2013/12/13/olmecas-serpientes-y-agua-la-venta-tabasco-mexico/ [Accessed 9 Sep. 2018].

Figure 45. Časopis Nova Akropola. (2016). Putovanje kroz vrijeme Maya. [online] Available at: https://nova-akropola.com/kulture-i-civilizacije/tragom-proslosti/putovanje-kroz-vrijeme-maya/ [Accessed 9 Sep. 2018].

Figure 46. The Event Chronicle. (2015). The mysterious "Gate of the Gods" at Hayu Marca, Peru» The Event Chronicle. [online] Available at: http://www.theeventchronicle.com/galactic/the-mysterious-gate-of-the-gods-at-hayu-marca-peru/ [Accessed 10 Sep. 2018].

Figure 47. Traveltipoffs.com. (2015). Turkey | travel tip offs. [online] Available at: http://www.traveltipoffs.com/category/europe/turkey/ [Accessed 10 Sep. 2018].

Figure 48. профиль, П. (2012). Рисунки на дольменах. Крест - звезда. [online] Isi-2025.blogspot.com. Available at: https://isi-2025.blogspot.com/2012/04/blog-post_10.html [Accessed 10 Sep. 2018].

Figure 49. Колтыпин, А. (2017). Д. Дмитриев, С. Фиалковская. Дольмены Кавказа: прикосновение к тайне жизни - Земля до потопа: исчезнувшие континенты и цивилизации. [online] Dopotopa.com. Available at: http://www.dopotopa.com/d_dmitriev_s_fialkovskaya_dolmeny_kavkaza_-_prikosnovenie_k_tayne_zhizni.html [Accessed 10 Sep. 2018].

Figure 50. Rabotni4ek.gallery.ru. (2008). Gallery.ru / Фото #29 - Лазаревское, сентябрь 2008 - rabotni4ek. [online] Available at: http://rabotni4ek.gallery.ru/watch?ph=wpj-TYW2 [Accessed 17 Sep. 2018]. (left). Nanoworld.org.ru. (2011). Бародинамика Шестопалова А.В. (Страница 55) — Формы, механизмы, энергия наномира — Форум лаборатории НАНОМИР. [online] Available at: http://nanoworld.org.ru/topic/126/page/55/ [Accessed 17 Sep. 2018]. (right).

Figure 51. Author archives.

Figure 52. Fedorov, A. Vlijanie geotektoniki na aktivnost' naselenija Kavkaza [The Influence of Geotectonics on the Activity of the Caucasus Population]. Almanac of Space and Time. Volume 2. No. 1. 2013.

Figure 53. Fedorov, A. Vlijanie geotektoniki na aktivnost' naselenija Kavkaza [The Influence of Geotectonics on the Activity of the Caucasus Population]. Almanac of Space and Time. Volume 2. No. 1. 2013.

Figure 54. Loza, B.

Figure 55. Easttennesseewildflowers.com. (2005). Rock layers like these can be found all along the highways in middle Utah. It is interesting to try to read the geologic layers. [online] Available at: http://www.easttennesseewildflowers.com/gallery3/index.php/Utah_2005/Rock_Layers [Accessed 25 Sep. 2018]. Dostoyanieplaneti.ru. (2016). Сырный камень на Бытхе - Достояние планеты. [online] Available at: http://dostoyanieplaneti.ru/3516-syrnyj-kamen-na-bytkhe [Accessed 10 Sep. 2018].

Figure 56. Privetsochi.ru. (2015). Дольмены. Как делали и подгоняли между собой плиты для строительства дольменов Кавказа. [online] Available at: http://privetsochi.ru/blog/history/51831.html [Accessed 25 Sep. 2018].

Figure 57. Galerie-laemmer.de. (2018). Galerie Laemmer – Experiments. [online] Available at: http://www.galerie-laemmer.de/experimente_en.html [Accessed 10 Sep. 2018].

Figure 58. Privetsochi.ru. (2015). Дольмены. Как делали и подгоняли между собой плиты для строительства дольменов Кавказа. [online] Available at: http://privetsochi.ru/blog/history/51831.html [Accessed 17 Sep. 2018].

Figure 59. Dushadolmena.ru. (2014). Душа дольмена :: Фотоальбом: У дольменов вдоль реки Ачибс. [online] Available at: http://dushadolmena.ru/f_arachibs.html [Accessed 10 Sep. 2018]. Sharikov, U. and Komissar, O. *Dol'meny Kavkaza. Geologicheskie aspekty I tehnologii stroitel'stva [Dolmens of the Caucasus. Geological Aspects and Technologies of construction].* (Krasnodar, 2011). p. 144.

Figure 60. Sharikov, U. and Komissar, O. *Dol'meny Kavkaza. Geologicheskie aspekty I tehnologii stroitel'stva [Dolmens of the Caucasus. Geological Aspects and Technologies of construction].* (Krasnodar, 2011). pp. 142,143.

Figure 61. Privetsochi.ru. (2016). Сад камней на горе Ландышевой. [online] Available at: http://privetsochi.ru/blog/walking/61913.html [Accessed 10 Sep. 2018]. Dolmen-kavkaz.ucoz.ru. (2011). Отчеты о посещениях дольменов - Страница 34 - Форум. [online] Available at: http://dolmen-kavkaz.ucoz.ru/forum/13-9-34 [Accessed 10 Sep. 2018].

Figure 62. Ordenxc.org. (2003). » Карачаево-Черкесская республика. Лесо-Кяфарь (Шпиль) ||| Орден Хранителей Смерти. [online] Available at: http://ordenxc.org/library/myortvye-goroda/karachaevo-cherkesskaya-respublika-leso-kyafar-shpil/ [Accessed 9 Sep. 2018].

Figure 63. Dolmen-kavkaz.ucoz.ru. (2011). Чашеобразные углубления (ЛУНКИ) - Форум. [online] Available at: http://dolmen-kavkaz.ucoz.ru/forum/4-25-1 [Accessed 10 Sep. 2018].

Figure 64. Present5.com. (2018). ПЕРВОБЫТНАЯ АРХИТЕКТУРА ПАЛЕОЛИТ Лёгкие наземные жилища. [online] Available at: http://present5.com/pervobytnaya-arxitektura-paleolit-lyogkie-nazemnye-zhilishha-2/ [Accessed 10 Sep. 2018].

Figure 65. Sharikov, U. and Komissar, O. *Dol'meny Kavkaza. Geologicheskie aspekty I tehnologii stroitel'stva [Dolmens of the Caucasus. Geological Aspects and Technologies of construction].* (Krasnodar, 2011). pp. 113,169.

Figure 66. Autor archive.

Figure 67. Loza, G.

Figure 68. Dolmen-kavkaz.ucoz.ru. (2012). технологические особености дольменов. - Страница 18 - Форум. [online] Available at: http://dolmen-kavkaz.ucoz.ru/forum/4-5-18 [Accessed 10 Sep. 2018].

Figure 69. Sharikov, U. and Komissar, O. *Drevnie tehnologii dol'menov Kavkaza*

[Ancient technologies of Caucuses dolmens]. (Krasnodar: 2008). pp. 29,32.

Figure 70. Dolmen.ucoz.ru. (2018). архитектурные особенности дольменов - Страница 45 - Форум. [online] Available at: http://dolmen.ucoz.ru/forum/2-25-45 [Accessed 10 Sep. 2018].

Figure 71. Колтыпин, А. (2018). Дольмены Кавказа. Конструкции дольменов (окрестности г.геленджик, Россия). Часть 3. Конструкции дольменов - Земля до потопа: исчезнувшие континенты и цивилизации. [online] Dopotopa.com. Available at: http://www.dopotopa.com/konstruktsii_dolmenov_gelendzhik_rossia.html [Accessed 24 Sep. 2018].

Figure 72. Paranormal-news.ru. (2012). В Краснодарском крае найден древний дольмен с каменным шаром. [online] Available at: http://paranormal-news.ru/news/v_krasnodarskom_krae_najden_drevnij_dolmen_s_kamennym_sharom/2012-06-08-4851 [Accessed 10 Sep. 2018].

Figure 73. Архитектура Сочи. (2016). Барельефная орнаментация плит дольменов — древнейшее монументальное искусство Кавказа. [online] Available at: https://arch-sochi.ru/2016/02/barelefnaya-ornamentatsiya-plit-dolmenov-drevneyshee-monumentalnoe-iskusstvo-kavkaza/ [Accessed 10 Sep. 2018].

Figure 74. Dolmen-kavkaz.ucoz.ru. (2017). Дольмены-монолиты - Форум. [online] Available at: http://dolmen-kavkaz.ucoz.ru/forum/13-803-1 [Accessed 25 Sep. 2018].

Figure 75. «Комсомольской правды», Я. (2016). Древнейшее в мире женское украшение сделали в Сибири 40 тысяч лет назад. [online] KP.KG - сайт «Комсомольской правды». Available at: https://www.kp.kg/daily/26384/3262813/ [Accessed 11 Sep. 2018]. (*left*). transients.info. (2016). Remote Viewing the Antikythera Mechanism: A Solution to an Engima | Daz Smith - transients.info. [online] Available at: http://www.transients.info/2016/06/remote-viewing-the-antikythera-mechanism-a-solution-to-an-engima-daz-smith/ [Accessed 11 Sep. 2018]. (right).

Figure 76. Uday-interesting.blogspot.com. (2010). Looking for a perfect mind relaxing leisure. [online] Available at: http://uday-interesting.blogspot.com/2010/04/ [Accessed 11 Sep. 2018].

Figure 77. En.wikipedia.org. (2018). Nias. [online] Available at: https://en.wikipedia.org/wiki/Nias [Accessed 11 Sep. 2018].

Figure 78. Séguin, X. (2013). The Vajra Of Indra - Eden Saga - english. [online] Eden Saga - english. Available at: http://eden-saga.com/en/vajra-thunder-diamond-symbol-of-enlightenment.html [Accessed 11 Sep. 2018].

Figure 79. https://commons.wikimedia.org/w/index.php?curid=8673555. Commons.wikimedia.org. (2018). File:Tláloc 3.jpg - Wikimedia Commons. [online] Available at: https://commons.wikimedia.org/wiki/

File:Tl%C3%A1loc_3.jpg [Accessed 11 Sep. 2018]. Png-library.com. (2018). Download Coat of arms of ukraine ukrainian soviet socialist embassy of ukraine #1382407 png. [online] Available at: https://png-library.com/png/coat-of-arms-of-ukraine-ukrainian-soviet-socialist-embassy-of-ukraine.html [Accessed 25 Sep. 2018].

Figure 80. Эзотерика. (2015). Яков Блюмкин ШАМБАЛА | Эзотерика. [online] Available at: http://ezoterik-page.com/yakov-blyumkin-shambala/ [Accessed 11 Sep. 2018].

Figure 81. Commons.wikimedia.org. (2018). File:Royal Crown of France.svg - Wikimedia Commons. [online] Available at: https://commons.wikimedia.org/wiki/File:Royal_Crown_of_France.svg [Accessed 11 Sep. 2018]. (left). Clipart-library.com. (2018). Free Prince Crown, Download Free Clip Art, Free Clip Art on Clipart Library. [online] Available at: http://clipart-library.com/prince-crown.html [Accessed 11 Sep. 2018]. (center). Commons.wikimedia.org. (2018). File:Dome of Saint Peter's Basilica (exterior).jpg - Wikimedia Commons. [online] Available at: https://commons.wikimedia.org/wiki/File:Dome_of_Saint_Peter%27s_Basilica_(exterior).jpg [Accessed 25 Sep. 2018].

Figure 82. Loza, B.

Figure 83. Het Hunebed Nieuwscafé. (2018). Hoe zijn de hunebedden gebouwd? - Het Hunebed Nieuwscafé. [online] Available at: https://www.hunebednieuwscafe.nl/2017/08/hoe-hunebedden-gebouwd/ [Accessed 11 Sep. 2018]. (left). Privetsochi.ru. (2015). Дольмены. Как перемещали многотонные плиты дольменов в древности. [online] Available at: http://privetsochi.ru/blog/history/51784.html [Accessed 11 Sep. 2018]. (right).

Figure 84. Kisspng.com. (2018). Baba Yaga Stock photography Cartoon Witchcraft - broom - Unlimited Download. Kisspng.com. [online] Available at: https://www.kisspng.com/png-baba-yaga-stock-photography-cartoon-witchcraft-bro-841751/download-png.html [Accessed 13 Sep. 2018].

Figure 85. Engineering, S. (2014). Edward Leedskalnin: A Book in Every Home. [online] Shamanic Engineering. Available at: http://www.shamanicengineering.org/edward-leedskalnin-a-book-in-every-home/ [Accessed 13 Sep. 2018].

Figure 86. THE KEELY MOTOR COMPANY. (2003). [online] Available at: https://www.lockhaven.edu/~dsimanek/museum/keely/keely.htm [Accessed 13 Sep. 2018].

Figure 87. Anon, (2017). [online] Available at: https://megalithica.ru/dolmen-prigorodnyi-2.html [Accessed 26 Sep. 2018]. (left). N, A. (2017). Дольмены. Часть 2. Как строились и зачем? Гипотезы. [online] Rgdn.info. Available at: https://rgdn.info/dolmeny._chast_2._kak_stroilis_i_

zachem_gipotezy [Accessed 17 Sep. 2018]. (right).

Figure 88. Loza, G.

Figure 89. Loza, G.

Figure 90. Dolmen-kavkaz.ucoz.ru. (2011). Чашеобразные углубления (ЛУНКИ) - Страница 11 - Форум. [online] Available at: http://dolmen-kavkaz.ucoz.ru/forum/4-25-11 [Accessed 13 Sep. 2018].

Figure 91. Extrim-centr.ru. (2018). Активный отдых. [online] Available at: https://extrim-centr.ru/ekskursii-abinskom-rajone/ [Accessed 13 Sep. 2018].

Figure 92. AnapaBest. (2017). Шапсуга – дольмены и ромашковые поля | AnapaBest. [online] Available at: https://www.anapabest.ru/guide/shapsuga-dolmenyi-i-romashkovyie-polya.html [Accessed 17 Sep. 2018].

Figure 93. Туризм, велосипеды, фитнес. (2011). Поход к морю через горы: Абинск-ст.Шапсугская-пос. Кабардинка. Часть вторая - Туризм, велосипеды, фитнес. [online] Available at: http://www.velotut.ru/2011/06/17/abinsk-kabarda2 [Accessed 13 Sep. 2018].

Figure 94. Туризм, велосипеды, фитнес. (2011). Поход к морю через горы: Абинск-ст.Шапсугская-пос. Кабардинка. Часть вторая - Туризм, велосипеды, фитнес. [online] Available at: http://www.velotut.ru/2011/06/17/abinsk-kabarda2 [Accessed 13 Sep. 2018].

Figure 95. Paranormal-news.ru. (2016). Место Силы: Шапсугский треугольник. [online] Available at: http://paranormal-news.ru/news/mesto_sily_shapsugskij_treugolnik/2016-11-01-12797 [Accessed 13 Sep. 2018]. (left) Megalithica.ru. (2017). Большой Шапсугский дольмен - MEGALITHICA.RU. [online] Available at: https://megalithica.ru/bolshoj-shapsugskij-dolmen.html [Accessed 13 Sep. 2018]. (right).

Figure 96. Anon, (2012). [online] Available at: http://www.neizvestniy-geniy.ru/cat/photo/rasten/595766.html [Accessed 26 Sep. 2018].

Figure 97. Шапсугский центр экологии, здоровья и отдыха. (2018). Достопримечательности. [online] Available at: http://shapsuga.net/main/1-dostoprimechatelnosti.html [Accessed 13 Sep. 2018].

Figure 98. Дольмены в Геленджике: загадка каменных склепов., Д. (2018). Дольмены в Геленджике: загадка каменных склепов. - humaninside. [online] humaninside. Available at: https://humaninside.ru/vokrug-nas/40612-dolmenyi_v_gelendjike_zagadka_kamennyih_sklepov.html [Accessed 13 Sep. 2018].

Figure 99. Megalithica.ru. (2017). Группа дольменов Пхабгучел - MEGALITHICA.RU. [online] Available at: https://megalithica.ru/gruppa-dolmenov-pxabguchel.html [Accessed 13 Sep. 2018].

Figure 100. Markovin, V. *Dol'meny Zapadnogo Kavkaza [Dolmens of the Western Caucasus]*. (Moscow, 1978), p. 139.

Figure 101. A Model for the Origin and Properties of Flicker-Induced Geometric Phosphenes. (2011). [online] Available at: https://www.ncbi. nlm.nih.gov/pmc/articles/PMC3182860/ [Accessed 13 Sep. 2018]. (*left*). Oubliette.org.uk. (1995). [online] Available at: http://www.oubliette.org. uk/Three.html [Accessed 13 Sep. 2018]. (*right*).

Figure 102. Zhezl.ucoz.ru. (2018). [online] Available at: http://zhezl.ucoz. ru/_ph/27/511650237.jpg [Accessed 14 Sep. 2018].

Figure 103. Nanoworld.org.ru. (2011). Бародинамика Шестопалова А.В. (Страница 7) — Формы, механизмы, энергия наномира — Форум лаборатории НАНОМИР. [online] Available at: http://nanoworld.org.ru/ topic/126/page/7/ [Accessed 14 Sep. 2018]. (*left*). "Дольмены В Поселке Джубга. Фонд Духовной Культуры.". 2016. New.Cosmoenergy.Ru. http://new.cosmoenergy.ru/photogallery/dolmeny_djubga.html. [Accessed 14 Sep. 2018]. (*right*).

Figure 104. Хеку, Н. (2015). Wall posts. [online] Vk.com. Available at: https:// vk.com/wall-47668002_3236 [Accessed 27 Sep. 2018]. (*left*). Dostoyanie-planeti.ru. (2017). Мегалиты села Хамышки - Достояние планеты. [online] Available at: http://dostoyanieplaneti.ru/362-mieghality-sie-la-khamyshki [Accessed 27 Sep. 2018]. (*right*).

Figure 105. Адыгские тамги. (2015). [online] Available at: http://egerukhay. ru/index/adygskie_tamgi/0-67 [Accessed 14 Sep. 2018].

Figure 106. Mpov.uw.edu.pl. (2012). Migration Period between Odra and Vistula - Runes/ runic alphabet. [online] Available at: http://www.mpov. uw.edu.pl/en/thesaurus/terms/runes-runic-alphabet- [Accessed 14 Sep. 2018].

Figure 107. Zombie-spl.narod.ru. (2007). Zombie-spl - походы выходного дня. [online] Available at: http://zombie-spl.narod.ru/walk/12-08-2007-lazarevskoe/18-08-2007-brnd/foto.html [Accessed 14 Sep. 2018]. (*left*). Gradvino.ru. (2016). Легенда о винограде и вине. [online] Available at: http://gradvino.ru/legenda_o_vinograde.html [Accessed 14 Sep. 2018]. (*right*).

Figure 108. Joy4mind.com. (2014). Мегалиты Краснодарского края. Дольмены поселка Новый | Неизведанное. [online] Available at: http://joy-4mind.com/?p=15982 [Accessed 14 Sep. 2018].

Figure 109. Joy4mind.com. (2014). Мегалиты Краснодарского края. Дольмены поселка Новый | Неизведанное. [online] Available at: http:// joy4mind.com/?p=15982 [Accessed 14 Sep. 2018].

Figure 110. Dolmen-kavkaz.ucoz.ru. (2011). Архив материалов - Дольмены Кавказа. [online] Available at: http://dolmen-kavkaz.ucoz.ru/news/?page4 [Accessed 14 Sep. 2018].

Figure 111. Artamonov, M. *Sokrovishha skifskih kurganov v sobranii*

Gosudarstvennogo Jermitazha [Treasures of the Scythian Barrows in the State Hermitage Museum]. (Praga – Leningrad,1966). Application I. Kronk.spb.ru. (2018). М.И. Артамонов, 1966. [online] Available at: http://kronk.spb.ru/library/artamonov-mi-1966-add2.htm [Accessed 26 Sep. 2018].

Figure 112. Dvernaya-moda.livejournal.com. (2015). Охотник на дольмены (урочище "Клады"). [online] Available at: https://dvernaya-moda.livejournal.com/114504.html [Accessed 14 Sep. 2018].

Figure 113. Национальный музей Республики Адыгея (Россия, Майкоп). (2014). [online] Available at: http://otzovik.com/review_738541.html [Accessed 14 Sep. 2018].

Figure 114. En.wikipedia.org. (2018). Newgrange. [online] Available at: https://en.wikipedia.org/wiki/Newgrange [Accessed 14 Sep. 2018].

Figure 115. Ru.wikipedia.org. (2018). Майкопская культура. [online] Available at: https://ru.wikipedia.org/wiki/%D0%9C%D0%B0%D0%B9%D0%BA%D0%BE%D0%BF%D1%81%D0%BA%D0%B0%D1%8F_%D0%BA%D1%83%D0%BB%D1%8C%D1%82%D1%83%D1%80%D0%B0 [Accessed 14 Sep. 2018]. Автор: Сергей 6662 - собственная работа, CC0, https://commons.wikimedia.org/w/index.php?curid=26005909.

Figure 116. Национальный музей Республики Адыгея (Россия, Майкоп). (2014). [online] Available at: http://otzovik.com/review_738541.html [Accessed 14 Sep. 2018].

Figure 117. Lovpache, N. *Drevnij Majkop [Ancient Maikop].* (Maikop, Publishing house of LLC "Ajax", 2008). pp. 28, 35.

Figure 118. Dostoyanieplaneti.ru. (2017). Идолы Урштена - Достояние планеты. [online] Available at: http://dostoyanieplaneti.ru/4730-doly-rushtena [Accessed 14 Sep. 2018].

Figure 119. Oursociety.ru. (2014). Надписи на Лооской плите рассказывают о загробном мире. [online] Available at: http://oursociety.ru/news/nadpisi_na_looskoj_plite_rasskazyvajut_o_zagrobnom_mire/2014-08-14-186 [Accessed 14 Sep. 2018].

Figure 120. «Готическое Таро Варго (The Gothic Tarot) - Форум О Таро И Оракулах». 2009. Tarot.My1.Ru. http://tarot.my1.ru/forum/6-343-1. [Accessed 14 Sep. 2018]. *(left)*. "Tarot - The Magician". 2007. Sublimeromance.Blogspot.Com. http://sublimeromance.blogspot.com/2007/04/tarot-magician.html. [Accessed 14 Sep. 2018]. *(right)*.

Figure 121. Yandex.ru. (2018). Из коллекции «Геленджик и его окрестности». [online] Available at: https://yandex.ru/collections/card/5b3cbf-0601d0cfbe8da1946e/ [Accessed 14 Sep. 2018].

Figure 122. Dolmen-kavkaz.ucoz.ru. (2015). знаки и символы на дольменах - Страница 18 - Форум. [online] Available at: http://dolmen-kavkaz.

ucoz.ru/forum/4-3-18 [Accessed 27 Sep. 2018].

Figure 123. Theladyinthegraveyard.tumblr.com. (2018). *Tumblr.* [online] Available at: https://theladyinthegraveyard.tumblr.com/ post/171101728399/compendium-maleficarums-demons [Accessed 14 Sep. 2018].

Figure 124. Photoshare.ru. (2008). *w3 - Warsow - Путешествия | photoshare.ru.* [online] Available at: http://photoshare.ru/photo1943428.html [Accessed 14 Sep. 2018].

Figure 125. «Заметки Практикующего Целителя -> Орбы – Развоплощенные Сущности». 2009. Lvovich.Ru. http://www.lvovich.ru/notebook/orbs2.shtml. [Accessed 14 Sep. 2018].

Figure 126. Kadykchanskiy.livejournal.com. (2014). Дольмены. ДНК - модуляторы?. [online] Available at: https://kadykchanskiy.livejournal.com/217706.html [Accessed 14 Sep. 2018].

Figure 127. Vantit.ru. (2007). Клады Воронеж. [online] Available at: http:// vantit.ru/antiquities/41-klady.html [Accessed 14 Sep. 2018].

Figure 128. Furduj, R. *Prelest' tajny – 2 [The charm of mystery – 2].* (Kiev, 2001). p. 180.

Figure 129. Loza, G.

Figure 130. Колтыпин, А. (2017). Д.Дмитриев, С.Фиалковская. Дольмены Кавказа: прикосновение к тайне жизни - Земля до потопа: исчезнувшие континенты и цивилизации. [online] Dopotopa.com. Available at: http://www.dopotopa.com/d_dmitriev_s_fialkovskaya_dolmeny_kavkaza_-_prikosnovenie_k_tayne_zhizni.html [Accessed 14 Sep. 2018].

Figure 131. Felitsin E. *Zapadno-Kavkazskie dol'meny [West Caucasian dolmens].* Materials on the archeology of the Caucasus. Release IX. (Moscow, 1904).

Figure 132. Felitsin E. *Zapadno-Kavkazskie dol'meny [West Caucasian dolmens].* Materials on the archeology of the Caucasus. Release IX. (Moscow, 1904).

Figure 133. Felitsin E. *Zapadno-Kavkazskie dol'meny [West Caucasian dolmens].* Materials on the archeology of the Caucasus. Release IX. (Moscow, 1904).

Figure 134. Felitsin E. *Zapadno-Kavkazskie dol'meny [West Caucasian dolmens].* Materials on the archeology of the Caucasus. Release IX. (Moscow, 1904).

Figure 135. Privetsochi.ru. (2015). Дольмены - ретроспектива. [online] Available at: http://privetsochi.ru/blog/history/52970.html [Accessed 14 Sep. 2018].

Figure 136. Privetsochi.ru. (2015). Дольмены - ретроспектива. [online] Available at: http://privetsochi.ru/blog/history/52970.html [Accessed 14

Sep. 2018].

Figure 137. Privetsochi.ru. (2015). Дольмены - ретроспектива. [online] Available at: http://privetsochi.ru/blog/history/52970.html [Accessed 14 Sep. 2018].

Figure 138. Privetsochi.ru. (2015). Дольмены - ретроспектива. [online] Available at: http://privetsochi.ru/blog/history/52970.html [Accessed 14 Sep. 2018].

Figure 139. Tourprom.ru. (2017). Фото Шуховская башня в Краснодаре | Краснодар, Россия | Турпром. [online] Available at: https://www.tourprom.ru/country/russia/krasnodar/attraction/shuhovskaya-bashnya-v-krasnodare/photos-shuhovskaya-bashnya-v-krasnodare/ [Accessed 26 Sep. 2018].

Figure 140. Ben, J. (2018). Nutria Rats In Louisiana | Nutria Rats. [online] Nutriarats.com. Available at: https://nutriarats.com/nutria-rats-in-louisiana/ [Accessed 27 Sep. 2018].

References

Introduction: Where It All Began

1. Jiri Hanzelka, and Miroslav Zikmund. Afrika grez i dejstvitel'nosti [Africa of dreams and reality]. (Moscow: Detgiz, 1958). This book has hundreds of black-and-white photographs. My grandparents had all three volumes of the Russian edition.
2. G.A. Menovshhikov. Chukotskie, korjakskie, jeskimosskie skazki [Fairy tales from Chukchis, Koryaks and Eskimos]. (Habarovsk, 1950).
3. L.A. Zenkevich. Zhizn' zhivotnyh [Life of Animals]. 6 vols. (7 books). (Moscow: Prosveshhenie, 1968 – 1971).
4. Biblioteka prikljuchenij [Library of adventure]. 20 vols. (Moscow: Detgiz, 1955 – 1959).
5. Wolfgang Crome. Urania Tierreich. 5 vols. (Leipzig, 1969).
6. Alexandra David-Neel. My Journey to Lhasa: The Classic Story of the Only Western Woman Who Succeeded in Entering the Forbidden City. (HarperCollins Publishers: 2005).
7. Arminius Vambery. Travels in Central Asia. (New York: Amo Press, 1970).
8. Burton Richard. Personal Narrative of a Pilgrimage to Al-Madinah and Meccah. (Dover Publications, Incorporated: 1964).
9. Semenov, S. Razvitie tehniki v kamennom veke [The development of technology in the Stone Age]. (Leningrad: Nauka, 1968). p. 230.

Part I

Dolmens: Ancient Mystic Megaliths

1. Oxford English Dictionary. "Dolmen". 1st edition. (Oxford, 1897).

2. Julia Valeva, Emil Nankov, and Denver Graninger. A Companion to Ancient Thrace. (John Wiley & Sons, 2015). p. 126.

3. Dmitriev, D. Dolmeny. Tajna Tysjacheleyij [Dolmens. The secret of the millennia]. October 2006. https://lah.ru/94dolmen/.

4. Furduj, R. Prelest' tajny – 2 [The charm of mystery – 2]. (Київ: Либідь, 2001). p. 169.

5. Tatiana Shnoorovozova. Tainstvennye mesta Rossii [Mysterious Places of Russia]. (Moscow: Olma Media Group, 2012). pp. 208-209.

6. Maria Pankova, Inga Eomanenko, Ilija Vagman and Olga Kuzmenko. 100 Znamenityh Zagadok Istorii [100 Famous Puzzles of History]. (Feniks, 2008). p. 30.

7. Furduj R. Prelest' tajny – 2 [The charm of mystery – 2]. (Київ: Либідь, 2001). p. 175.

8. Ibid. p. 175.

9. Ibid. p. 170.

10. Neapolitansky, S. and Matveev, S. Sakral'naja arhitektura mira [Sacred Architecture of the World]. (Amrita Rus, 2013). p. 194.

11. Vladimir Yashkardin. "Dolmens. Pamjati Vladimira Ivanovicha Markovina [In memory of Vladimir Ivanovich Markovin]". 2014. http://www.softelectro.ru/dolmen.html.

12. Kudin, M. "Dol'meny i ritual [Dolmens and ritual]". Sochi, Sochi Local Ethnographer, Issue 4, 1999. p. 1.

13. Ibid. p. 1.

14. Lavrov L. "Dol'meny Severo-Zapadnogo Kavkaza [Dolmens of the North-West Caucasus]". Proceedings of Ablyali, Sukhumi, volume 31, 1960. p. 104.

Who Built the Dolmens

1. Formozov A. Pamjatniki pervobytnogo iskustva na territorii SSSR [Monuments of primitive art on the territory of the USSR]. (Moscow: Nauka, 1966). p. 89.

2. Sharikov, U. and Komissar, O. Drevnie tehnologii dol'menov Kavkaza [Ancient technologies of Caucuses dolmens]. (Krasnodar: Sovet. Kuban', 2011). pp. 4-5.

3. Steblin-Kamensky, M. Mif [Myth]. (Leningrad: Nauka, 1976). p. 38.

4. Ibid. p. 38.

5. Blavatsky E. The people of the Blue Mountains. (Wheaton, Illinois: Theosophical Press, 1922).

6. Yaroslav Pytlyvij. "Krymskie sledy Chernomorskogo potopa [Crimean Traces of the Black Sea Flood]". On-line magazine "Telegraf". No. 394. Sep. 2, 2016. http://ktelegraf.com. ru/8388-krymskie-sledy-chernomorskogo-potopa.html.

7. Sharikov, U. and Komissar, O. Drevnie tehnologii dol'menov Kavkaza [Ancient technologies of Caucuses dolmens]. (Krasnodar: Sovet. Kuban', 2008). p. 9.

8. Shnoorovozova T. Tainstvennye mesta Rossii [Mysterious places of Russia]. (Moscow: Olma Media Group, 2012). p. 208.

9. Peter Simon Pallas. Travels through the Southern Provinces of the Russian Empire, in the Years 1793 and 1794. (London: John Stockdale, 1812).

10. Dubois de Montpérreux, Frédéric. Voyage autour du Caucase, chez les Tcherkesses et les Abkhases, en Colchide, en Géorgie, en Arménie et en Crimée, 6 volumes and 5 atlases. (Paris: Librairie De Gide, 1839). Image from 5*2, Ser4-XXX, fig 5-7), https://archive.org/details/voyageautourduc08montgoo.

11. Formozov, A. Pamjatniki pervobytnogo issustva na territorii SSSR [Monuments of primitive art on the territory of the USSR]. (Moscow: Nauka, 1966). p. 90.

12. Vladimir Yashkardin. "Dolmens. Pamjati Vladimira Ivanovicha Markovina [In memory of Vladimir Ivanovich Markovin]". 2014.

http://softelectro.ru/dolmen.html.

13. Markovin, V. Dol'meny Zapadnogo Kavkaza [Dolmens of the Western Caucasus]. (Moscow: Nauka, 1978). p. 60.

14. Vladimir Yashkardin. "Dolmens. Pamjati Vladimira Ivanovicha Markovina [In memory of Vladimir Ivanovich Markovin]". 2014. http://softelectro.ru/dolmen.html.

15. Blavatsky, H. The Secret Doctrine. Vol. II. (London: The Theosophical Publishing Company, 1888). p. 343 https://www.theosociety.org/pasadena/sd-pdf/SecretDoctrineVol2_eBook.pdf.

16. Gennadii Eremin. "Svjazhi solnce kamennoj cep'ju… [Tie the sun with a stone chain …]". Magazine "Technique - Youth", No. 6. 1979. http://www.fantclubcrimea.info/2-eremin.html.

17. Loodmila Shaposhnikova. Tajna plemeni Golubyh gor [The Mystery of the Tribe of the Blue Mountains]. (Moscow: Nauka, 1969).

18. Akaba, L. Iz mifologii Abhazov [From the mythology of the Abkhazians]. (Sukhumi: Alashara, 1976). p. 10 and 14.

19. David Hatcher Childress. Lost Cities Series. (Adventures Unlimited Press, 1986-2009).

Why the Dolmens Were Built

1. Leila Sabzali. Otkrovenija sakral'nogo Gobustana [Revelations of sacred Gobustan]. (Baku: Apostroph, 2010). p. 2.

2. Aseev, A. "O megaliticheskih sooruzhenijah drevnego mira [About megalithic constructions of the ancient world]". Journal of Occultism and Yoga, No. 52. 1972. p. 109.

3. Vladimir Megre. Zvenjashhie kedry Rossii [Ringing cedars of Russia]. (Moscow-Saint Petersburg. 1996 – 2010).

4. Klein, L. Drevnie migracii i proishozhdenie indoevropejskih narodov [Ancient migrations and the origin of the Indo-European peoples]. (Saint Petersburg, 2007). p. 16.

5. Ibid. p. 40.

6. Dunaevskaya, I. O strukturnom shodstve hattskogo jazyka s jazykami Severo-Zapadnogo Kavkaza [On the structural similarity

of the Hutt language with the languages of the northwestern Caucasus]. Collection in honor of Academician N.A .Orbeli. (Moscow-Leningrad, 1960).

7. Vinayak Bharne and Krupali Krusche. Rediscovering the Hindu Temple: The Sacred Architecture and Urbanism of India. (UK: Cambridge Scholar Publishing, 2014). p. 83.

8. Johnson, W. A dictionary of Hinduism. (Oxford University Press, 2009). Online version. http://www.oxfordreference. com/view/10.1093/acref/9780198610250.001.0001/acref-9780198610250-e-2801.

9. Jones C. and Ryan J. Encyclopedia of Hinduism. (Facts on File, 2006). pp. 156-157.

10. Aeschylus. Prometheus Bound, trans. Herbert Weir Smyth. (Harvard University Press, 1926).

11. Ibid.

12. Jacob W. Pascheles. Sippurim. (Prague: W. Pascheles, 1870). pp. 51-52.

13. Jose Argüelles. The Mayan Factor: Path Beyond Technology. (Bear and Company, 1987). p. 61.

14. Asya Pereltsvaig. Languages of the World. (Cambridge University Press, 2012). p. 196.

15. Thor Heyerdahl. The Maldive Mystery. (Adler & Adler, 1986).

16. Podosinov, A. Ex oriente lux! Orientacija po stranam sveta v arhaicheskih kul'turah Evrazii [Ex oriente lux! Orientation according to the countries of light in the archaic cultures of Eurasia]. (Moscow: Jazyki russkoj kul'tury, 1999). p. 583.

17. Martin P. Nilsson. The Minoan-Mycenaean Religion and Its Survival in Greek Religion. (Biblo-Moser,1950). p. 421. "there is a widespread opinion that the equal-limbed cross is another symbol of the sun."

18. Emma Lila Fundaburk, Mary Douglass Fundarburk Foreman and Vernon James Knight Jr. Sun Circles and Human Hands. (University Alabama Press, 2001).

19. Teshev M. Otchet "Raskopki megaliticheskogo arhitekturnogo kompleksa Psynako-1 v 1985 g. [Report. Excavations of the megalithic architectural complex of Psynako 1 in 1985]". Archive of the IA RAS. P-1 No. 11097.

20. Kondrjakov V. "O dol'menah eshhe raz [About dolmens again]". Newspaper "Shapsugia". May 19, 1993.

21. Miller, A. "Razvedki na Chernomorskom poberezh'e Kavkaza v 1907 g. [Intelligence on the Black Sea Coast of the Caucasus in 1907]". News of the Archaeological Commission. Vol. 33, St. Petersburg, 1909.

22. Danilenko, V. and Shilov, U. Nachala civilizacii: Kosmogonija pervobytnogo obshhestva [The beginning of civilization. Cosmogony of primitive society]. (Moscow: Delovaja kniga. Raritet, 1999).

23. James P. and Torp N. Tajny drevnih civilizacij [Mysteries of ancient civilizations]. (Moscow: Eksmo, 2001).

24. Teshev, M. "Megaliticheskij arhitekturnyj kompleks Psynako-1 v Tuapsinskom rajone [Megalithic architectural complex of Psynako 1 in the Tuapse area]". (Maykop : Archeology of Adygea, 1988). p. 147.

25. Fedorov A. "Vlijanie geotektoniki na aktivnost' naselenija Kavkaza [The Influence of Geotectonics on the Activity of the Caucasus Population]". Almanac of Space and Time. Volume 2. No. 1. 2013.

26. Byakov A. and Pytunin M. Geofizicheskie issledovanija dol'menov Kavkaza [Geophysical studies of dolmens of the Caucasus]. http:// dolmen-kavkaz.ucoz.ru/news/geofizicheskie_issledovanija_dolmenov_kavkaza/2011-09-28-30. 2011.

27. Furdui, R. and Shvaydak, U. Prelest' tajny [The Charm of Mystery]. (Kiev: Lybid', 1992). p. 22.

28. Nikita Kondryakov. "Tajny sochinskih dol'menov [Secrets of the Sochi dolmens]". 2002. http://dolmen-kavkaz.ucoz.ru/BOOK.pdf.

29. Fedorov, A. "Vlijanie geotektoniki na aktivnost' naselenija Kavkaza [The Influence of Geotectonics on the Activity of the Caucasus Population]". Almanac of Space and Time. Volume 2. No. 1. 2013.

30. Ibid.

31. Chernyavsky, G., Skrebushevsky, B., and Skripachev, V. "Bortovaja apparatura kosmicheskich apparatov monitoringa predvestnikov zemletrjasenij [Onboard equipment of spacecraft for monitoring earthquake precursors]". Issledovanija Zemli iz kosmosa [Earth Exploration from Space]. N 6. 2004. pp. 50-58.

32. Fedorov, A. "Vlijanie geotektoniki na aktivnost' naselenija Kavkaza [The Influence of Geotectonics on the Activity of the Caucasus Population]". Almanac of Space and Time. Volume 2. No. 1. 2013.

33. Dubrov A. Geomagnitnoe pole i zhizn' [The Geomagnetic field and Life]. (Leningrad: Gidrometeoizdat, 1974).

34. Ibid.

35. Fedorov, A. "Vlijanie geotektoniki na aktivnost' naselenija Kavkaza [The Influence of Geotectonics on the Activity of the Caucasus Population]". Almanac of Space and Time. Volume 2. No. 1. 2013.

36. Marie D. Jones and Larry Flaxman. Mind Wars: A History of Mind Control, Surveillance, and Social Engineering by the Government, Media, and Secret Societies. (New Page Books, 2015).

37. Justesen, D. "Microwaves and behaviour". American Psychologist, Volume 30(3). March 1975. p. 396.

38. Alunathemovie.com. (2014). Aluna the Movie. [online] Available at: http://www.alunathemovie.com/ [Accessed 9 Sep. 2018].

39. Ivan Efremov. Lezvie britvy [Razor blade]. (Moscow: Pravda, 1963). p. 424.

40. Mantak Chia. Darkness Technology. Darkness Techniques for Enlightenment. Thailand. pp. 3,16. https://www.universal-tao.com/products/darkness_technology.html.

How the Blocks Were Quarried and Processed

1. Sharikov, U. and Komissar, O. Drevnie tehnologii dol'menov Kavkaza [Ancient technologies of Caucuses dolmens]. (Krasnodar: Sovet. Kuban', 2008). p. 11.

2. Ibid. p. 14.

3. Mary Gage. The Art of Splitting Stone: Early Rock Quarrying Methods in Pre-Industrial New England 1630-1825. 2nd Edition. (Amesbury, MA: Powwow River Books, 2005).

4. Galerie-laemmer.de. (2018). Galerie Laemmer – Experiments. [online] Available at: http://www.galerie-laemmer.de/experimente_en.html [Accessed 10 Sep. 2018].

5. Percy Fawcett. Journey to the Lost City of Z. (New York: Overlook Press, 2010). pp. 76-77.

6. Ben Bendig. "Could Ancient Peruvians Soften Stone?" Epoch Times. 2013. Updated May 22, 2016. https://www.theepochtimes.com/could-ancient-peruvians-soften-stone_291849.html.

7. Davidovits J., Francisco A. "Fabrication of stone objects, by geopolymeric synthesis, in the pre-Incan Huanaka civilization (Peru)". Paper presented at the 21st International Symposium for Archaeometry Brookhaven National Laboratory. (New-York, 1981). p. 21.

8. Ibid.

9. Yaroslav Putlivij. "Plastilinovye dol'meny [Plasticine dolmens]". Crimean Telegraph. No. 402. October 28. 2016. http://ktelegraf.com.ru/8563-plastilinovye-dolmeny.html.

10. Ibid.

11. Sharikov, U. and Komissar, O. Drevnie tehnologii dol'menov Kavkaza [Ancient technologies of Caucuses dolmens]. (Krasnodar: Sovet. Kuban', 2008). p. 32.

12. Semenov, S. Prehistoric Technology: An Experimental Study of the Oldest Tools and Artifacts from Traces of Manufacture and Wear, trans. M. W. Thompson. (London: Cory, Adams & Mackay, 1964).

13. Ibid. p. 66.

14. Semenov, S. Razvitie tehniki v kamennom veke [The development of technology in the Stone Age]. (Leningrad: Nauka, 1968). p. 81.

15. Engelbach, R. The problem of the obelisks, from a study of the unfinished obelisk at Aswan. (T. Fisher Unwin, 1923). p. 36.

16. Louis Ginzberg. The Legends of the Jews. 7 volumes. (The Jewish

Publication Society of America, 1969).

17. Ibid.

18. azdoc.pl. (2018). Collected Essays by Immanuel Velikovsky - PDF Free Download. [online] Available at: https://azdoc.pl/collected-essays-by-immanuel-velikovsky.html [Accessed 10 Sep. 2018].

19. Kizilov, A. (2016). Barel'efnaja ornamentacija plit dol'menov — drevnejshee monumental'noe iskusstvo Kavkaza [Bas-relief Ornamentation of Slabs of Dolmens: The Most Ancient Monumental Art of the Caucasus]. [online] Архитектура Сочи. Available at: https://arch-sochi.ru/2016/02/barelefnaya-ornamentatsiya-plit-dolmenov-drevneyshee-monumentalnoe-iskusstvo-kavkaza/ [Accessed 10 Sep. 2018].

Transporting the Megalithic Blocks

1. Umansky A. Spravochnik proektirovshhika raschetno-teoreticheskij [Handbook of theoretical calculations of the designer]. (Moscow: Stroiizdat, 1972). p. 104.

2. Markovin, V. SPUN - doma karlikov: Zametki o dol'menah Zapadnogo Kavkaza [Ispun – dwarfs' houses: Notes of dolmens of Western Caucasus]. (Krasnodar: Knizhnoe izdatel'stvo, 1985). p. 61.

3. Sharikov, U. and Komissar, O. Drevnie tehnologii dol'menov Kavkaza [Ancient technologies of Caucuses dolmens]. (Krasnodar: Sovet. Kuban', 2008). p. 20.

4. "ARCHEOLOGICAL PAPERS OF THE AMERICAN ANTHROPO-LOGICAL ASSOCIATION". Vol. 20, Issue 1, ISSN 1551-823X. pp. 17–32.

5. Graham Hancock. The Sign and the Seal: The Quest for the Lost Ark of the Covenant. (New York: Simon & Schuster,1993). p. 308.

6. Friedrich Otto Hultsch Pappus. Pappi Alexandrini collectionis quae supersunt. (Apud Weidmannos, 1877).

7. Sanskrit-lexicon.uni-koeln.de. (2008). Monier Williams Online Dictionary. [online] Available at: http://www.sanskrit-lexicon.uni-koeln.de/monier/ [Accessed 10 Sep. 2018].

How the Blocks Were Lifted

1. Semenov, S. Razvitie tehniki v kamennom veke [The development of technology in the Stone Age]. (Leningrad: Nauka, 1968). p. 230.
2. Theodore Illion. In Secret Tibet. (Adventures Unlimited Press, 1991).
3. Andrew Collins. Gods of Eden: Egypt's Lost Legacy and the Genesis of Civilization. (Headline Publishing Group, 1998). p. 60.
4. Ibid. p. 83.
5. Liz Norton. Aspects of Ecphrastic Technique in Ovid's Metamorphoses. (Cambridge Scholars Publishing, 2013). p. 115.
6. Isaac Cory. Cory's Ancient Fragments of the Phoenician, Carthaginian, Babylonian Egyptian and Other Authors. (London: Reeves & Turner, 1876). p. 13.
7. Rt.com, (2014). Sound wave 3Dvolution: Japanese scientists move objects using acoustic levitation. [online] Available at: https://www.rt.com/news/3d-japan-objects-levitation-102/ [Accessed 11 Sep. 2018].
8. Choi, C. (2006). Scientists Levitate Small Animals. [online] Live Science. Available at: https://www.livescience.com/1165-scientists-levitate-small-animals.html [Accessed 11 Sep. 2018].
9. David Hatcher Childress. Anti-Gravity and the World Grid. (Adventures Unlimited Press, 1987). pp. 213-214.
10. Blavatsky, H. The Secret Doctrine: Anthropogenesis. (Theosophical Publishing Society, 1893). p. 148.
11. Patrick J. Kelly. Practical Guide to "Free-Energy" Devices. Version 33.0. 2018. Ch. 11. p. 8. http://www.free-energy-info.com/PJKbook.pdf. [Accessed 20 March. 2018].
12. Handwerk, B. "Antigravity Machine Patent Draws Physicists' Ire". National Geographic News. Nov. 11, 2005. [Accessed 10 May. 2017]. https://news.nationalgeographic.com/news/2005/11/1111_051111_junk_patent.html.
13. Patrick J. Kelly. Practical Guide to "Free-Energy" Devices. Version 33.0. 2018. Ch. 11. p. 9. http://www.free-energy-info.com/PJKbook.pdf. [Accessed 20 March. 2018].

14. Masaru Emoto. Messages from Water. Vol. 1. (Hado Publishing, 1999).

Part II

Enigmas and Unexplained Phenomena

1. Science Astronomy. (2017). Nemesis Star Theory: The Sun's 'Death Star' Companion. [online] Space.com. Available at: https://www. space.com/22538-nemesis-star.html [Accessed 11 Sep. 2018].
2. Zecharia Sitchin. The 12th Planet. (Avon, 1976).
3. Markovin, V. Dol'meny Zapadnogo Kavkaza [Dolmens of the Western Caucasus]. (Moscow: Nauka, 1978). p. 139.

Puzzles of the Dolmens Signs and Symbols

1. Wikipedia, The Free Encyclopedia, s.v. "Phosphene," (accessed May 2, 2018). https://en.wikipedia.org/w/index.php?title=Phosphene&oldid=828999368.
2. MichaelRule, Matthew Stoffregen and Bard Ermentrout. "A Model for the Origin and Properties of Flicker-Induced Geometric Phosphenes". PLOS. Computational Biology. Sep 29, 2011. https://www.ncbi.nlm.nih.gov/pmc/articles/PMC3182860/.
3. Suzanne Carr. Entoptic Phenomena. (MA dissertation, 1995). (Accessed May 10, 2018). http://www.oubliette.org.uk/Three.html.
4. Ibid.
5. Jearl Walker. The Amateur Scientist: About Phosphenes: patterns that appear when the eyes are closed. (Scientific American, 1981). pp. 142-152.
6. Bryan Hillard. Futhark: Mysterious Ancient Runic Alphabet of Northern Europe. June 18, 2015. (Accessed May 12, 2018). https://www.ancient-origins.net/artifacts-ancient-writings/futhark-mysterious-ancient-runic-alphabet-northern-europe-003250.

7. Giles N. Odin's Runes: The Definitive Rune Handbook. (Starburst Publishing, 2013). p. 19.

8. Paul Rhys Mountfort. Nordic Runes: Understanding, Casting, and Interpreting the Ancient Viking Oracle. (Inner Traditions, 2003). p. 19.

Mysterious Artifacts and Geological Formations

1. Kudin, M. Kalendarnye motivy v kul'ture dol'menov [Calendar Motifs in Dolmen Culture]. Sochi. 2005. pp. 6-7. (Accessed May 23, 2018) http://www.softelectro.ru/dolmen_048_010.pdf.

2. Ibid.

3. Ibid.

4. Ibid.

5. Artamonov, M. Sokrovishha skifskih kurganov v sobranii Gosudarstvennogo Jermitazha [Treasures of the Scythian Barrows in the State Hermitage Museum]. (Praga – Leningrad, 1966). Application I.

6. Turchaninov, G. Pamjatniki pis'ma i narodov Kavkaza i Vostochnoj Evropy [Monuments of the Letter and Language of the Peoples of the Caucasus and Eastern Europe]. (Leningrad, 1971). pp. 11-33.

7. Lovpache, N. Drevnij Majkop [Ancient Maikop]. (Maikop, Publishing house of LLC "Ajax", 2008). p. 91.

8. Ibid. pp. 28, 35.

9. Daur, R. Cherkesskaja kalligrafija. Mifojepicheskie alfavity (abhazo-adygskaja jazykovaja sem'ja) [Circassian calligraphy. Mythopoeia alphabets (Abkhaz-Adyghe language family)]. 2011. (Accessed June 10, 2018). http://apsnyteka.org/1356-daur_cherkesskaya_kalligrafiya.html.

10. Yuga.ru (2014). "Uchenyj iz Adygei rasshifroval nadpisi o zagrobnom mire na Looskoj plite bronzovogo veka [A Scientist from Adygea Deciphered Inscriptions about the Afterlife on the Loo Plate

of the Bronze Age]". [online]. Available at: https://www.yuga.ru/news/340667/ [Accessed May 12, 2018].

Dolmen Power

1. Furdui, R. and Shvaydak, U. Prelest' tajny [The Charm of Mystery]. (Kiev: Lybid', 1992). p. 31.

2. Volkova, E. and Valganov, S. Dol'menu. O zagadke Dol'menov [Dolmens. The Riddle about Dolmens]. 2008. http://polet-dushi.ru/osnovy-zhizni/dolmeny-o-zagadke-dolmenov/?_utl_t=tb.

3. D. Verishchagin, D. and Titov, K. Jegregory chelovecheskogo mira. Logika i navyki vzaimodejstvija [Egregors of the human world. Logic and interaction skills]. (St. Petersburg, Athena Publishing House, 2008). p. 99.

4. Maria Pankova, Inga Eomanenko, Ilija Vagman and Olga Kuzmenko. 100 Znamenityh Zagadok Istorii [100 Famous Puzzles of History]. (Feniks, 2008). p. 60.

5. Wikipedia, The Free Encyclopedia, s.v. "Backscatter (photography)," (accessed September 2, 2018). https://en.wikipedia.org/wiki/Backscatter_(photography)

Dolmen Healing and Spirituality

1. Furduj, R. Prelest' tajny – 2 [The charm of mystery – 2]. (Київ: Либідь, 2001). p. 172.

2. Robins D. "The Dragon Project and the Talking Stones." New Scientist. Oct. 21, 1982. pp. 166-168, 170-171.

3. Furduj, R. Prelest' tajny – 2 [The charm of mystery – 2]. (Київ: Либідь, 2001). p. 175

4. Ibid. p. 176.

5. Ibid.

6. Vartanyan, I. and Tsirulnikov, E. Kosnut'sja nevidimogo, uslyshat' neslyshimoe [Touch invisible, hear inaudible]. (Leningrad: Akademia Nauk SSSR, 1985). p. 74.

7. Ibid.

8. Furduj, R. Prelest' tajny – 2 [The charm of mystery – 2]. (Київ: Либідь, 2001).

9. Vernadskij, V. "Neskol'ko slov o noosfere [A few words about the noosphere]". Uspehi sovremennoj biologii [Success of the modern biology]. Number. 18. Issue. 2. (Moscov: Nauka, 1944). pp. 113—120.

10. Gennadii Eremin. "Svjazhi solnce kamennoj cep'ju… [Tie the sun with a stone chain ...]". Magazine "Technique - Youth", No. 6. 1979. http://www.fantclubcrimea.info/2-eremin.html.

11. Attuned Vibrations. (2018). What are the Solfeggio frequencies? | Attuned Vibrations. [online] Available at: https://attunedvibrations.com/solfeggio/ [Accessed 16 Sep. 2018].

12. Royal Rife machine. (2014). Royal Rife machine. [online] Royal-rife-machine.com. Available at: http://www.royal-rife-machine.com/ [Accessed 16 Sep. 2018].

13. Furduj, R. Prelest' tajny – 2 [The charm of mystery – 2]. (Київ: Либідь, 2001). p. 180.

14. Nikonov, V. and Trost', D. (2018). Дольмены – статья [Dolmens – article]. [online] Yugzone.ru. Available at: http://www.yugzone.ru/articles/613 [Accessed 16 Sep. 2018].

15. Dushadolmena.ru. (2016). Dusha dol-mena :: Glavnaja [Dolmen soul :: Major]. [online] Available at: http://dushadolmena.ru/ [Accessed 16 Sep. 2018].

Part III

Lost Dolmens

1. Formozov A. Pamjatniki pervobytnogo iskustva na territorii SSSR [Monuments of primitive art on the territory of the USSR]. (Moscow: Nauka, 1966). pp. 97-98.

2. Felitsin E. "Zapadno-Kavkazskie dol'meny [West Caucasian dolmens]". Materials on the archeology of the Caucasus. Release IX. (Moscow, 1904).

3. Ibid.

4. Yashkardin, V. (2017). Lekcija N0. 4. Dol'meny megaliticheskoj civilizacii [Lecture #4. Dolmens of a megalithic civilization]. [online] Softelectro.ru. Available at: http://softelectro.ru/dolmen2/dolmen2.html [Accessed 16 Sep. 2018].

5. Aseev, A. "O megaliticheskih sooruzhenijah drevnego mira [About megalithic constructions of the ancient world]". Journal of Occultism and Yoga, No. 52. 1972. p. 109.

6. Felitsyn, E. Kubanskie drevnosti [Ancient Kuban]. (Ekaterinodar, 1879). p. 13.

7. Ibid.

Appendix 2: Getting the Most from Your Trip

1. Alison Tilley and Ben Wicks. Tilley Travel Tips for Safe Easy Worry-free Travelling (Revised). (Alison Tilley Productions, 1994).

Index

About the Author

Boris Loza was born in Krasnodar, North Caucasus, and his various interests have brought him recognition in a variety of fields. From being a winner at the first international Cyber Security Contest and publishing articles in magazines for elite hackers to writing travel articles and developing innovative computer technologies for his private companies, Dr. Loza always finds time for his true passion—traveling around the world. He writes in Russian and English and is a scholar of megaliths found in his extensive travel adventures.

Loza's interest in history, megalithic structures, and alternative archaeology began when his daughter presented him with one of Zecharia Sitchin's books about ancient astronauts. From Easter Island, Egypt, and India to Ethiopia, Tibet, and Colombia, and many other exotic destinations, Loza tries to find his own answers to questions about our ancient past. He is not afraid to offer "politically incorrect" theories and explanations "forbidden" by mainstream academic disciplines.

In this book, Loza presents his firsthand account of unique megalithic structures—the dolmens scattered around the area where he used to live. He presents information about the first attempts to study dolmens and fascinating theories of who, when, how, and for what purpose these unique structures were built. Also, this book discusses areas that are not well traveled as well as tips for planing an exotic trip to see the dolmens.

Find out how to use dolmen power to heal yourself and change your perception about these artifacts left by ancient people. Learn about alternative history and archaeology, something that you will never find in schoolbooks!

ANCIENT TECHNOLOGY IN PERU & BOLIVIA
By David Hatcher Childress

Childress speculates on the existence of a sunken city in Lake Titicaca and reveals new evidence that the Sumerians may have arrived in South America 4,000 years ago. He demonstrates that the use of "keystone cuts" with metal clamps poured into them to secure megalithic construction was an advanced technology used all over the world, from the Andes to Egypt, Greece and Southeast Asia. He maintains that only power tools could have made the intricate articulation and drill holes found in extremely hard granite and basalt blocks in Bolivia and Peru, and that the megalith builders had to have had advanced methods for moving and stacking gigantic blocks of stone, some weighing over 100 tons.

340 Pages. 6x9 Paperback. Illustrated.. $19.95 Code: ATP

HIDDEN FINANCE, ROGUE NETWORKS & SECRET SORCERY
The Fascist International, 9/11, & Penetrated Operations
By Joseph P. Farrell

Pursuing his investigations of high financial fraud, international banking, hidden systems of finance, black budgets and breakaway civilizations, Farrell investigates the theory that there were not *two* levels to the 9/11 event, but *three*. Farrell unravels the many layers behind the 9-11 attack, layers that include the Deutschebank, the Bush family, the German industrialist Carl Duisberg, Saudi Arabian princes and the energy weapons developed by Tesla before WWII.

296 Pages. 6x9 Paperback. Illustrated. $19.95. Code: HFRN

THRICE GREAT HERMETICA AND THE JANUS AGE
By Joseph P. Farrell

What do the Fourth Crusade, the exploration of the New World, secret excavations of the Holy Land, and the pontificate of Innocent the Third all have in common? Answer: Venice and the Templars. What do they have in common with Jesus, Gottfried Leibniz, Sir Isaac Newton, Rene Descartes, and the Earl of Oxford? Answer: Egypt and a body of doctrine known as Hermeticism. The hidden role of Venice and Hermeticism reached far and wide, into the plays of Shakespeare (a.k.a. Edward DeVere, Earl of Oxford), into the quest of the three great mathematicians of the Early Enlightenment for a lost form of analysis, and back into the end of the classical era, to little known Egyptian influences at work during the time of Jesus.

354 Pages. 6x9 Paperback. Illustrated. $19.95. Code: TGHJ

COVERT WARS AND BREAKAWAY CIVILIZATIONS
By Joseph P. Farrell

Farrell delves into the creation of breakaway civilizations by the Nazis in South America and other parts of the world. He discusses the advanced technology that they took with them at the end of the war and the psychological war that they waged for decades on America and NATO. He investigates the secret space programs currently sponsored by the breakaway civilizations and the current militaries in control of planet Earth. Plenty of astounding accounts, documents and speculation on the incredible alternative history of hidden conflicts and secret space programs that began when World War II officially "ended."

292 Pages. 6x9 Paperback. Illustrated. $19.95. Code: BCCW

THE MYSTERY OF THE OLMECS
by David Hatcher Childress

The Olmecs were not acknowledged to have existed as a civilization until an international archeological meeting in Mexico City in 1942. Now, the Olmecs are slowly being recognized as the Mother Culture of Mesoamerica, having invented writing, the ball game and the "Mayan" Calendar. But who were the Olmecs? Where did they come from? What happened to them? How sophisticated was their culture? Why are many Olmec statues and figurines seemingly of foreign peoples such as Africans, Europeans and Chinese? Is there a link with Atlantis? In this heavily illustrated book, join Childress in search of the lost cities of the Olmecs! Chapters include: The Mystery of Quizuo; The Mystery of Transoceanic Trade; The Mystery of Cranial Deformation; more.

296 PAGES. 6x9 PAPERBACK. COLOR SECTION. $20.00. CODE: MOLM

IN SECRET MONGOLIA
by Henning Haslund

Haslund takes us into the barely known world of Mongolia of 1921, a land of god-kings, bandits, vast mountain wilderness and a Russian army running amok. Starting in Peking, Haslund journeys to Mongolia as part of a mission to establish a Danish butter farm in a remote corner of northern Mongolia. With Haslund we meet the "Mad Baron" Ungern-Sternberg and his renegade Russian army, the many characters of Urga's fledgling foreign community, and the last god-king of Mongolia, Seng Chen Gegen, the fifth reincarnation of the Tiger god and the "ruler of all Torguts." Aside from the esoteric and mystical material, there is plenty of just plain adventure: Haslund encounters a Mongolian werewolf; is ambushed along the trail; escapes from prison and fights terrifying blizzards; more.

374 PAGES. 6x9 PAPERBACK. ILLUSTRATED. BIBLIOGRAPHY & INDEX. $16.95. CODE: ISM

MEN & GODS IN MONGOLIA
by Henning Haslund

Haslund takes us to the lost city of Karakota in the Gobi desert. We meet the Bodgo Gegen, a god-king in Mongolia similar to the Dalai Lama of Tibet. We meet Dambin Jansang, the dreaded warlord of the "Black Gobi." Haslund and companions journey across the Gobi desert by camel caravan; are kidnapped and held for ransom; witness initiation into Shamanic societies; meet reincarnated warlords; and experience the violent birth of "modern" Mongolia.

358 PAGES. 6x9 PAPERBACK. ILLUSTRATED. INDEX. $18.95. CODE: MGM

BIGFOOT NATION
A History of Sasquatch in North America
By David Hatcher Childress

Long-time cryptozoology researcher David Hatcher Childress takes us on a tour of Bigfoot Nation—the apparently real world of bigfoot around us in the United States and Canada. Surviving in the shadows and suffering from loss of habitat, bigfoot has had many encounters with humans, many of which are chronicled here. In these meetings, bigfoot has been found to be curious, dangerous and even amorous, depending on the circumstances. He appears in commercials and movies, on roadside billboards and stamps. In fact, bigfoot is everywhere, trying to maintain his lifestyle on the fringes of modern society, and gently creeping into our dreams.

320 Pages. 6x9 Paperback. Illustrated. $22.00. Code: BGN

TECHNOLOGY OF THE GODS
The Incredible Sciences of the Ancients
by David Hatcher Childress

Popular *Lost Cities* author David Hatcher Childress takes us into the amazing world of ancient technology, from computers in antiquity to the "flying machines of the gods." Childress looks at the technology that was allegedly used in Atlantis and the theory that the Great Pyramid of Egypt was originally a gigantic power station. He examines tales of ancient flight and the technology that it involved; how the ancients used electricity; megalithic building techniques; the use of crystal lenses and the fire from the gods; evidence of various high tech weapons in the past, including atomic weapons; ancient metallurgy and heavy machinery; the role of modern inventors such as Nikola Tesla in bringing ancient technology back into modern use; impossible artifacts; and more.

356 PAGES. 6x9 PAPERBACK. ILLUSTRATED. BIBLIOGRAPHY. $16.95. CODE: TGOD

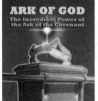

ARK OF GOD
The Incredible Power of the Ark of the Covenant
By David Hatcher Childress

Childress takes us on an incredible journey in search of the truth about (and science behind) the fantastic biblical artifact known as the Ark of the Covenant. This object made by Moses at Mount Sinai—part wooden-metal box and part golden statue—had the power to create "lightning" to kill people, and also to fly and lead people through the wilderness. The Ark of the Covenant suddenly disappears from the Bible record and what happened to it is not mentioned. Was it hidden in the underground passages of King Solomon's temple and later discovered by the Knights Templar? Was it taken through Egypt to Ethiopia as many Coptic Christians believe? Childress looks into hidden history, astonishing ancient technology, and a 3,000-year-old mystery that continues to fascinate millions of people today. Color section.

420 Pages. 6x9 Paperback. Illustrated. $22.00 Code: AOG

LOST CONTINENTS & THE HOLLOW EARTH
I Remember Lemuria and the Shaver Mystery
by David Hatcher Childress & Richard Shaver

A thorough examination of the early hollow earth stories of Richard Shaver and the fascination that fringe fantasy subjects such as lost continents and the hollow earth have had for the American public. Shaver's rare 1948 book *I Remember Lemuria* is reprinted in its entirety, and the book is packed with illustrations from Ray Palmer's *Amazing Stories* magazine of the 1940s. Palmer and Shaver told of tunnels running through the earth—tunnels inhabited by the Deros and Teros, humanoids from an ancient spacefaring race that had inhabited the earth, eventually going underground, hundreds of thousands of years ago. Childress discusses the famous hollow earth books and delves deep into whatever reality may be behind the stories of tunnels in the earth. Operation High Jump to Antarctica in 1947 and Admiral Byrd's bizarre statements, tunnel systems in South America and Tibet, the underground world of Agartha, the belief of UFOs coming from the South Pole, more.

344 PAGES. 6x9 PAPERBACK. $16.95. CODE: LCHE

LOST CITIES & ANCIENT MYSTERIES OF THE SOUTHWEST
By David Hatcher Childress

Join David as he starts in northern Mexico and then to west Texas amd into New Mexico where he stumbles upon a hollow mountain with a billion dollars of gold bars hidden deep inside it! In Arizona he investigates tales of Egyptian catacombs in the Grand Canyon, cruises along the Devil's Highway, and tackles the century-old mystery of the Lost Dutchman mine. In California Childress checks out the rumors of mummified giants and weird tunnels in Death Valley—It's a full-tilt blast down the back roads of the Southwest in search of the weird and wondrous mysteries of the past!

486 Pages. 6x9 Paperback. Illustrated. $19.95. Code: LCSW

AXIS OF THE WORLD
The Search for the Oldest American Civilization
by Igor Witkowski

Witkowski's research reveals remnants of a high civilization that was able to exert its influence on almost the entire planet, and did so with full consciousness. Sites around South America show that this was a place where they built their crowning achievements. Easter Island, in the southeastern Pacific, constitutes one of them. The Rongo-Rongo language that developed there points westward to the Indus Valley. Taken together, the facts presented provide new proof that an antediluvian civilization flourished several millennia ago.

220 pages. 6x9 Paperback. Illustrated. $18.95. Code: AXOW

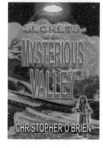

SECRETS OF THE MYSTERIOUS VALLEY
by Christopher O'Brien

No other region in North America features the variety and intensity of unusual phenomena found in the world's largest alpine valley, the San Luis Valley of Colorado and New Mexico. Since 1989, O'Brien has documented thousands of high-strange accounts that report UFOs, ghosts, crypto-creatures, cattle mutilations, and more, along with portal areas, secret underground bases and covert military activity. Hundreds of animals have been found strangely slain during waves of anomalous aerial craft sightings. Is the government directly involved? Are there underground bases here?

460 PAGES. 6x9 PAPERBACK. ILLUSTRATED. BIBLIOGRAPHY. $19.95. CODE: SOMV

PIRATES & THE LOST TEMPLAR FLEET
by David Hatcher Childress

The lost Templar fleet was originally based at La Rochelle in southern France, but fled to the deep fiords of Scotland upon the dissolution of the Order by King Phillip. This banned fleet of ships was later commanded by the St. Clair family of Rosslyn Chapel. St. Clair and his Templars made a voyage to Canada in the year 1398 AD, nearly 100 years before Columbus! Chapters include: 10,000 Years of Seafaring; The Templars and the Assassins; The Lost Templar Fleet and the Jolly Roger; Maps of the Ancient Sea Kings; Pirates, Templars and the New World; Christopher Columbus—Secret Templar Pirate?; Later Day Pirates and the War with the Vatican; Pirate Utopias and the New Jerusalem; more.

320 PAGES. 6x9 PAPERBACK. ILLUSTRATED. BIBLIOGRAPHY. $16.95. CODE: PLTF

ORDER FORM

**10% Discount
When You Order
3 or More Items!**

One Adventure Place
P.O. Box 74
Kempton, Illinois 60946
United States of America
Tel.: 815-253-6390 • Fax: 815-253-6300
Email: auphq@frontiernet.net
http://www.adventuresunlimitedpress.com

ORDERING INSTRUCTIONS

✓ Remit by USD$ Check, Money Order or Credit Card

✓ Visa, Master Card, Discover & AmEx Accepted

✓ Paypal Payments Can Be Made To:

   info@wexclub.com

✓ Prices May Change Without Notice

✓ 10% Discount for 3 or More Items

SHIPPING CHARGES

United States

✓ Postal Book Rate { $4.50 First Item
                     50¢ Each Additional Item

✓ POSTAL BOOK RATE Cannot Be Tracked!
   Not responsible for non-delivery.

✓ Priority Mail { $6.00 First Item
                  $2.00 Each Additional Item

✓ UPS { $7.00 First Item
        $1.50 Each Additional Item

   NOTE: UPS Delivery Available to Mainland USA Only

Canada

✓ Postal Air Mail { $15.00 First Item
                    $3.00 Each Additional Item

✓ Personal Checks or Bank Drafts MUST BE
   US$ and Drawn on a US Bank

✓ Canadian Postal Money Orders OK

✓ Payment MUST BE US$

All Other Countries

✓ Sorry, No Surface Delivery!

✓ Postal Air Mail { $19.00 First Item
                    $7.00 Each Additional Item

✓ Checks and Money Orders MUST BE US$
   and Drawn on a US Bank or branch.

✓ Paypal Payments Can Be Made in US$ To:
   info@wexclub.com

SPECIAL NOTES

✓ RETAILERS: Standard Discounts Available

✓ BACKORDERS: We Backorder all Out-of-
   Stock Items Unless Otherwise Requested

✓ PRO FORMA INVOICES: Available on Request

✓ DVD Return Policy: Replace defective DVDs only

ORDER ONLINE AT: www.adventuresunlimitedpress.com

**10% Discount When You Order
3 or More Items!**

Please check: ✓

☐ This is my first order   ☐ I have ordered before

Name	
Address	
City	
State/Province	Postal Code
Country	
Phone: Day	Evening
Fax	Email

Item Code	Item Description	Qty	Total

Please check: ✓

	Subtotal ▶	
	Less Discount-10% for 3 or more items ▶	
☐ Postal-Surface	Balance ▶	
☐ Postal-Air Mail (Priority in USA)	Illinois Residents 6.25% Sales Tax ▶	
	Previous Credit ▶	
☐ UPS (Mainland USA only)	Shipping ▶	
	Total (check/MO in USD$ only) ▶	

☐ Visa/MasterCard/Discover/American Express

Card Number:

Expiration Date: Security Code:

✓ SEND A CATALOG TO A FRIEND: